The Right to Narcissism

The Right to Narcissism

A CASE FOR AN IM-POSSIBLE SELF-LOVE

PLESHETTE DeARMITT

FORDHAM UNIVERSITY PRESS

New York 2014

Library of Congress Cataloging-in-Publication Data

DeArmitt, Pleshette, 1967–
    The right to narcissism : a case for an im-possible self-love /
Pleshette DeArmitt. — First edition.
        pages cm
    Includes bibliographical references and index.
    ISBN 978-0-8232-5443-9 (cloth : alk. paper) —
    ISBN 978-0-8232-5444-6 (pbk. : alk. paper)
    1. Narcissism.   I. Title.
    BF575.N35D4 2014
    128—dc23
                                        2013015248

Printed in the United States of America

16 15 14   5 4 3 2 1

First edition

for Kas,
my traveling companion

Contents

Acknowledgments

During the writing of this book, which spanned more years than I anticipated, I experienced, like Narcissus, death and (re)birth, mourning and renewal. This work is intellectually and affectively shaped by the untimely loss of each of my parents and the joyous arrival of the ardent Seraphine Pari, allowing me to think through the limits and expansiveness of narcissism, as well as narcissism's inextricable relationship to love of the other.

While writing this book, I enjoyed the friendship and support of colleagues, friends, and family who, directly and indirectly, contributed to this project coming to fruition. I would like to express my gratitude to those colleagues in the field who invited me to share my work in speech and in print, as well as to those who provided important feedback, encouragement, and friendship: Tina Chanter, Crina Gschwandtner, Martin Hägglund, Leonard Lawlor, Dawne McCance, Elizabeth Rottenberg, Alan Schrift, and Ewa Ziarek. I am especially grateful to Elissa Marder and Kelly Oliver for the intellectual and emotional generosity each has shown me over the last few years. Michael Naas, a dear friend and mentor, has without a doubt profoundly marked the course of my thinking and writing, for which I am deeply appreciative.

I greatly benefitted from the Professional Development Assignment (2010–11) granted to me by the University of Memphis, which enabled me to make important strides in completing my manuscript. I am thankful to my colleagues and graduate students in the Philosophy Department at Memphis for their helpful feedback on early versions of chapters that were presented in our Research in Progress series. I am also grateful to the graduate students in my Rousseau seminar on the passions for their careful and challenging engagement with the material, which sharpened my own interpretations. Finally, I would like to extend my sincere thanks to my chair, Deborah Tollefsen, for her support during the completion of this work and for making the Memphis Philosophy Department a more family-friendly environment.

I would like to express my deep appreciation to my editor, Helen Tartar, for her generous support of my manuscript, and to Tom Lay, for his tremendous care and efficiency in assisting this first-time book author. I also would like to thank Juliann Barbato for her judicious and skillful copy editing, and Eric Newman for his patient help in the publication of this work.

I am truly grateful to Billy Zane for kindly granting me permission to use his elegant and spare portrayal of Echo and Narcissus on the cover of my book.

For their energy, joie de vivre, and friendship, I am indebted to Justine Malle and Joanne Molina. Finally, I thank my family, Sally and Jerry Aron, Manouchehr and Mastaneh Saghafi, Dara Saghafi and Yoli Rodriquez, for their love and support over the years. The memory of my mother, Dolores DeArmitt, accompanied me during the writing of this book.

Early versions of a few sections of the book were previously published. I am grateful to the presses for granting me permission to republish them here in revised form. An abbreviated version of Chapter 3 first appeared as "On the Border between

Abjection and the Third: The (Re)Birth of Narcissus in the Works of Julia Kristeva" in *Between Revolt and Affect: The Unstable Boundaries of Kristeva's Polis*, edited by Tina Chanter and Ewa Ziarek (Albany: State University of New York Press, 2005). A section of Chapter 5 was first published as "The Impossible Incorporation of Narcissus: Mourning and Narcissism in Derrida" in *Philosophy Today*, 44, Supplement, Selected Studies in Phenomenology and Existential Philosophy (2000): 84–90. A version of Chapter 6 previously appeared as "Resonances of Echo: A Derridean Allegory" in *Mosaic* 41, no. 3 (2009): 89–100.

The Right to Narcissism

Introduction: The Right to Narcissism?

The right to narcissism must be rehabilitated, it needs the time and the means.
[*Le droit au narcissisme doit être rehabilité, il y faut le temps et les moyens.*]
   —Jacques Derrida, *Right of Inspection*

The right to narcissism? Any claim to a right to narcissism would raise more than a few eyebrows. Is not narcissism problematic enough, but to call for its legitimation, to openly declare, as Derrida does in the above epigraph, that narcissism should be "rehabilitated," as if it has ever been neglected and fallen into disrepair?[1] Have not our contemporary philosophers, cultural theorists, theologians, and even literary scholars spilled much ink over the pervasive egoism of our time and, with it, the troubling disregard for the other—each and every other? Have not ethical discourses proliferated as correctives to this seemingly intractable problem? In fact, is not Derrida one of those who has addressed this very problem and done so in the most trenchant manner by exposing that the whole of the Western tradition is fueled by a powerful narcissistic fantasy of self-return, whether it goes by the name "presence," "auto-affection," "phal-logocentrism," or, most recently, "sovereignty"? What, then, are we to make of Derrida's seemingly anomalous positive invocation of narcissism and his provocative appeal to rehabilitate the right to it?

This book was inspired by and takes up Derrida's challenge to radically rethink the concept of narcissism and, thus, begins the work of rehabilitating this notion by patiently reexamining the terms and figures that have been associated with it. In the three parts that follow, we will sketch out the adventures of self-love in the works of Jean-Jacques Rousseau, Julia Kristeva, and Jacques Derrida—three great thinkers of "narcissism." Each, in his or her own idiom and context, profoundly grapples with the complexity of what has been gathered under the terms "self-love" (*amor sui, amour de soi, amour-propre*) and its younger relative "narcissism," which only entered our vocabulary in the late nineteenth century and belongs to a medicalized discourse, specifically that of psychoanalysis and psychiatry.[2]

Of course, one might counter that each of these thinkers has so persuasively charted out the profound moral, psychological, political, and even metaphysical violence that is wrought as a consequence of the workings of narcissism that a deconstruction of this notion would be virtually impossible or, at the very least, undesirable. We will make the case, admittedly an unconventional and perhaps an unpopular one, that a rethinking and reinscription of narcissism is not only possible but also vitally necessary in order to address the very problems of what is commonly associated with the term "narcissism"—solipsism, egoism, ipseity, in other words, a pathological self-return, a phantasmatic circularity that dreams of self-enclosure and unleashes a cruel violence on both the "other" and the "self." Indeed, not one of these thinkers would deny that what has been called "narcissism" (or, in the case of Rousseau, *amour-propre*) is of the utmost concern and, as described above, must be condemned in no uncertain terms.

However, if we could claim that there is a single lesson concerning narcissism to be learned from these thinkers, it would be that, as Derrida writes in *H. C. for Life, That Is to Say . . .* , "[n]arcissism has no contrary, no other side, no beyond, and love for the other, respect for the other, self-denial in favor of the other do not interrupt any narcissistic movement."[3] If this is the case, and we will contend that it is, then one cannot simply deny or dispense with narcissism, one cannot occupy a position of non-narcissism, and to attempt to occupy such a position would even be perilous. For a naïve notion of narcissism—that is, one that believes that this term merely designates a moral failing or a pathology that can be condemned, corrected, cured, or simply denied—reduces narcissism to a mere state or condition that afflicts an already constituted subject and thus fails to truly reckon with the structures of narcissism. If life is lived, as these thinkers show, "in accordance with originary narcissism," then the movement and structures of life itself and with it the "self" and "other" must be radically rethought. Thus, before we take the time to acquire the means to rehabilitate narcissism by unfolding Rousseau, Kristeva, and Derrida's extensive and nuanced meditations on the subject, often interpreting their accounts through and with the insights of psychoanalysis, we will begin with three "scenes" in which a *certain* right to narcissism is claimed. The following scenes will seem to suggest that these thinkers, in fact, cannot provide us with the resources to rework narcissism but rather offer us only unequivocal critiques and condemnations of such a dangerous auto-affection. It will be the burden of this book to show otherwise.

ROUSSEAU AND THE RIGHT TO REGARD, OR THE ORIGIN OF INEQUALITY

Rousseau famously opens Part II of the *Second Discourse* by dramatically depicting the moment that society, and with it inequality, is inaugurated among men.[4]

> The first man who, having enclosed a piece of ground, to whom it occurred to say this is mine and found people sufficiently simple to believe him, was the true founder of civil society. How many crimes, wars, murders, how many miseries and horrors Mankind would have been spared by him who, pulling up the stakes or filling in the ditch, had cried out to his kind: Beware of listening to the impostor. (SD 170/OC III:164)

This transformative scene, which stands in stark relief to the static and relatively peaceful state of nature that preceded it, does not arise, however, out of nowhere but is prepared for by numerous changes in man's existence and character.[5] For the idea of property, a concept that requires a notion of one's own and a belief in possessing the right to it, "depending as it does on many prior ideas which could only arise successively, did not take shape all at once in man's mind" (SD 170/OC III:164). Rather, Rousseau argues that a great distance in human history had to be traversed, "industry and enlightenment acquired," before humans would enter civil society with all its attendant problems (SD 170/OC III:164). In his analyses of the sea shifts that humankind undergoes in the course of historical development, Rousseau often "cover[s] multitudes of Centuries in a flash" (SD 173/OC III:167). However, let us linger on a few of those moments in which man's self-regard and the way that he views others is transformed.

In his natural state, Rousseau tells us, "[m]an's first sentiment was that of his existence, his first care that of his preservation" (SD 170/OC III:164).[6] In this premoral state, primitive man was guided by two wholly natural principles: self-love (*amour de soi*), or an innate concern for one's own well-being, and compassion (*pitié*), or an instinctual aversion to the suffering of other sentient beings. Thus, savage man, prior to the birth of reflection in him, was solitary and benign. Yet, circumstances—terrain, climate, seasons, and interactions with animals and other humans—altered his natural mode of existence and hence his very nature.

It was first man's competition with animals for the fruits of nature and his need to protect himself from the ferocity of those beasts which threatened his life that brought about a decisive change in his constitution. In his repeated interactions with animals, man began to discern differences between them, those of size, shape, velocity, temperament, and so on. By attending to these differences, a form of reflection that developed almost automatically, what Rousseau calls "a mechanical prudence [*une prudence machinale*]," was produced in man (SD

171/OC III:165). Despite the rudimentary and mechanistic nature of this reflection, man had begun to separate himself from animals, as "this new enlightenment that resulted from this development increased his superiority over the other animals" (SD 171/OC III:165).

The nascent ability to distinguish between qualities and relations allowed man to put this knowledge to work for his profit: "He learned to set traps for [animals], he tricked them in a thousand ways, and [. . .] in time he became the master [*le maître*] of those that could be of service to him and the scourge of those that could harm him (SD 171/OC III:165–66). Man's newly developed intellectual abilities, specifically the emergence of a kind of cunning intelligence, allowed him to master and menace those who were his superior physically. From mere mechanical reflection, from which he learned to discriminate between differences of relation (fast/slow, strong/weak, etc.), man's eyes were opened to a new type of relation—superior/inferior. Although it was prudence that moved man to compare himself with his fellow animals, pride was its result. Rousseau describes man's new regard for himself as follows:

> That is how his first look at himself [*le premier regard qu'il porta sur lui-même*] aroused the first movement of pride in him; that is how, while he was as yet scarcely able to discriminate ranks, and considered himself in the first rank as a species [*au premier par son espèce*], he was from afar preparing to claim first rank as an individual [*il se préparoit de loin à y prétendre par son individu*]." (SD 172/OC III:166)

Rousseau portrays man's first look at himself vis-à-vis other animals as the cause of the first movement of pride in his heart. This "species pride," which made man claim for himself first place among animals, laid the foundations for his entry into the social world of men and served as a template for his future claims to be ranked first among his kind.

Some distance must still be traversed to arrive at the "right to regard" that, on Rousseau's account, will be the source of "inequality and vice" (SD 175/OC III:169). While primitive man came to regard himself as master of the animal world, man *qua* man (i.e., as a social being) was still unknown to him. With time, he began to comprehend the actions and motivations of his own species. "Taught by experience that love of well-being [*l'amour du bien-être*] is the sole spring of human actions," he acquired the ability to differentiate the occasions "when common interest should make him count on the help of his kind, and the even rarer occasions when competition should make him suspicious of them" (SD 172/OC III:166). Despite this emerging ability to identify with his own kind, man's linguistic capacities, Rousseau tells us, were scarcely more advanced than those of animals, and as such his interactions with other men remained presocial.

It was not until "the period of a first revolution," during which families and communal dwellings were established, that "a sort of property" arose and with it discord (SD 173/OC III:167). Rousseau's text, however, does not allow us to attribute the degeneration of man's nature to the formation of property per se. Rather, "the mind and the heart [must] grow active" before property as such can become a source of inequality and strife (SD 175/OC III:169). This new arrangement, where the social takes root, created the conditions in which new ideas and sentiments could take shape, which, in Rousseau's narrative, irrevocably alters human nature.

Living in proximity to one another and enjoying newfound leisure, individuals had occasion "to attend to different objects and to make comparisons" between men, as their ancestors had first done with animals (SD 175/OC III:169). This attention to differences of kind and relation gave rise to new ideas—those of "merit and of beauty which produce sentiments of preference" (SD 175/OC III:169). Indeed, each began to regard the other anew, with eyes that are opened to the social for the first time.

> Everyone began to look at everyone else and to wish to be looked at himself [*Chacun commença à regarder les autres et à vouloir être regardé soi-même*], and public esteem acquired a value. The one who sang and danced the best; the handsomest, the strongest, the most skillful, or the most eloquent came to be the most highly regarded [*le plus consideré*] and this was the *first step at once toward inequality*

and vice; from these preferences arose vanity [*la vanité*] and contempt on one hand, shame and envy on the other.[7] (SD 175/OC III:169–70, emphasis mine)

This new regard for others, which assesses and ranks qualities, which gives preference to some and not to others, in turn gave rise to the desire to be regarded and esteemed. For, Rousseau writes, "[a]s soon as men had begun to appreciate one another and the idea of regard had taken shape in their mind (*l'idée de la considération fut formée dans leurs esprit*), everyone claimed a right to it (*chacun prétendit y avoir droit*)" (SD 175/OC III:170).

Rousseau skillfully links the formation of the "idea of regard" with the claim to the *right* to be (well) regarded. In fact, one might legitimately argue that the right to property as such is nothing but an extension of this earlier demand or claim to narcissism—that is, to the right to be ranked first as a species and then as an individual. Is it not precisely the awakening of the "right to regard" in *The Discourse on the Origin of Inequality* that gives rise to vanity and envy, the source of the corruption of man's natural self-love, *amour de soi*, perverting it and producing its pathological substitute—*amour-propre*? Indeed, was it not Rousseau who served as a cultural canary in the mine about the pervasive dangers of the awakening of *amour-propre* and the degenerative effects of this variant of "narcissism"? Yet, this is only one version of Rousseau's famous morality tale. What if there were another in which *amour-propre* is transformed into a virtue, reconciling a right to self-love with sociality and justice?

KRISTEVA AND THE RIGHT TO ONE'S OWN,
OR THE CULT OF ORIGINS

In her 1990s text *Nations without Nationalism*, Kristeva addresses the complexity of one's origins, as she had done in *Strangers to Ourselves*, in terms of ethnic, racial, and national roots, especially in the context of European nation-states.[8] What is of concern to us here is not her arguments for or against particular visions for or configurations of nations (e.g., Montesquieu's *l'esprit général* vs. Herder's *Volksgeist*); rather it is her portrayal of a *collective narcissism* that serves as a kind of founding principle for many a state or people. In sketching out this "cult of origins," which involves a *double hatred*—of others and of oneself—that is all too often at the root of social and political formations, Kristeva evokes a well-known scene from Freud's earliest text on the formation of society. She writes:

> Freud had demonstrated to what extent the conglomeration of men and women into sets is oppressive and death-bearing. "Society is founded on a common crime," he wrote in *Totem and Taboo*, and the exclusion of "others," which binds the identity of a clan, sect, party, or nation, is equally the source of the pleasure of identification ("this is what *we* are, therefore this is what *I* am") and of barbaric persecution ("that is foreign to me, therefore I throw it out, hunt it down, or massacre it"). (50)

While the story of patricide and the fraternal pact may set the scene for Kristeva's analysis of the logic of the clan or the tribe, her account appears to be more indebted to another Freudian narrative, which is perhaps less famous but no less fundamental and powerful. Specifically, we are referring to the phenomenon of "the narcissism of minor or small differences [*Narzißmus der kleinen Unterschiede*]" that Freud employs to describe ethnic, racial, and religious conflicts between peoples who are very proximate to one another, geographically and genetically, yet they regard one another as foreign and hostile.

Sharing with Freud a belief in the existence and power of the death drives (which are frequently manifested as hatred, aggression, and cruelty), Kristeva seems to take up and put to work Freud's assertion in *Group Psychology and the Analysis of the Ego* that "[i]n the undisguised antipathies and aversions which people feel towards strangers with whom they have to do [*sic*] we may recognize the expression of self-love [*Selbstliebe*]—of narcissism."[9] In fact, the source of what Kristeva is calling "the cult of origins," in its various guises, is a certain narcissism—a paranoid and defensive self-love that seeks to protect itself at all costs. But protect itself against what aggression or harm? "This self-love," Freud explains, "works for the preservation of the individual, and behaves as though the occurrence of any divergence from his own particular lines of development involved a criticism of them and a demand for their alteration" (SE 18:102).

From this point of view, any encounter with others whose lines of development diverge from one's own is perceived by the self (collective or individual) as both a critical judgment and a threat. Paradoxically, this narcissism, which imagines itself to be threatened, effectively turns into a "hatred of oneself" and, as Kristeva suggests, "withdraw[s] into a sullen, warm private world, unnameable and biological, the impregnable 'aloofness' of a weird primal paradise—family, ethnicity, nation, race" (NWN 3). This "hatred of oneself," which seeks solace and safety in one's own, also gives rise to "a defensive hatred" that is easily transformed into "a persecuting hatred" of those "who do not share my origins and who affront me personally, economically, and culturally" (NWN 2–3). This insecure and paranoid narcissism, which Freud terms "the narcissism of minor differences" and Kristeva "the cult of origins," fuels an obsessive "worship of one's 'very own,' of which the 'national' is the collective configuration, the *common denominator* that we imagine we have as 'our own,' precisely, along with other 'own and proper' people like us" (NWN 51). Of course, shoring up this (very fragile) narcissism to which the collective self so desperately clings in the name of some right of blood or patrimony is an inexhaustible and impossible task. The purity of and pride in one's own—"the narcissistic excitement of rediscovering strengthened, superegotic, hyperbolic 'ideals' "—can only be established and "maintained" through ritual sacrifice of what is deemed to fall outside of the proper, "of which the aggressive, paranoid excesses are well known" (NWN 52).

While it may seem that Kristeva condemns this claim to a right to *one's own* exclusively in terms of nationalist and racist ideologies, she is equally critical in this text and throughout her writings of any cult of origins, under any name or banner. For example, in *Nations without Nationalism*, she worries that in its struggles against racism and xenophobia the French movement SOS Racisme also slips into a kind of all-encompassing, oceanic narcissism. Even the most well-meaning groups or movements (including feminist movements) may take flight into a state of narcissistic fusion that promises "the delight of being on a boundless ocean," running the risk of totalizing and totalitarian trends (NWN 51). Indeed, Kristeva shows no sympathy for any expression of the cult of origins and thus for the narcissism that fuels it. Countering the innumerable demands, from all sides, for a right to one's own, Kristeva calls for a "recognition of otherness," which ought to be "a right and a duty for everyone," citizen and foreigner alike (NWN 31). Yet, must the respect for otherness foreclose any relation to "one's own" and what is proper to the self?[10] Kristeva, as we will see, will offer another narrative about narcissism, one in which a right to a healthy self-love would not be opposed to a right to otherness.[11]

DERRIDA AND THE RIGHT TO THE SOVEREIGN SELF, OR THE PHANTASM OF NARCISSISM

In *Rogues: Two Essays on Reason*, Derrida, in one of his last works, powerfully takes on the narcissistic phantasm of the sovereign self.[12] After sketching out the etymology of the self, Derrida writes:

> But do we really need etymology when simple analysis would show the possibility of power and possession in the mere positioning of the self as oneself [*soi-même*], in the mere self-positioning of the self as properly oneself? The first turn or first go around of circularity or sphericity comes back round or links back up, so to speak, with itself, with the same, the self, and with the proper of oneself [. . .]. The turn makes up the whole and makes a whole with itself.[13]

While reading *Rogues*, it is easy to become convinced that Derrida's earlier declaration that the right to narcissism ought to be rehabilitated could not possibly hold true for his thought more generally. For in this text, he seems to be returning to and circling around concerns that preoccupied him throughout his entire career; that is, to a certain "rotary motion of some quasi-circular return or rotation toward the self, toward the origin itself, toward and upon the self of the origin" (10/30). In fact, Derrida links this circular or spherical movement with what should be interpreted as a narcissistic movement, if narcissism is understood, as André Green describes it in *Life Narcissism, Death Narcissism*, as the "Desire for the One," for a "unitary utopia, an ideal totalization."[14]

How exactly does this impossible, phantasmatic desire for the One give rise to a certain right to narcissism? Derrida turns our attention to two intersecting and inseparable aspects of "the history of humanity": on the one hand, the invention of the "wheel" and, on the other hand, "the history of the rights of 'man'" (R 10/30). By superimposing the history of the Western subject onto the turning of the wheel, Derrida reveals the circular or spherical trajectory of a self that attempts to return to itself "in a specular, self-designating, sovereign, and autotelic fashion" (R 10/30). This rotary movement of the self toward its own origin, "toward the origin itself," aims at sovereign self-determination, that is, at "the autonomy of the *ipse*" (R 10/30). "By *ipseity*," Derrida is "suggest[ing] some 'I can,' or at the very least the power that gives itself its own law, its force of law, its self-representation, the sovereign and reappropriating gathering self" (R 11/30). This "I can" of the *ipse* thus signals not only an ability or power to act but also a freedom "to do as one pleases, to decide, to choose, to determine oneself, to be master, and first of all master of oneself [*d'être maître et d'abord maître de soi*]" (R 22–3/45). Therefore, the desire for the origin, for the One, Derrida shows, is inseparable from a powerful dream of autonomy in which the "I" wants to be the master of itself. And, to truly be master of oneself, one must solely give oneself the law in a movement "of sovereign self-determination" (R 10/30).

This narcissistic circuit of self-return, which Derrida has so often exposed, analyzed, and criticized, not only belongs to the history of the philosophical subject but also to that of the democratic citizen who recognizes himself first and foremost as a subject of rights. He argues that "the history of the rights of 'man,' beginning with the right to recognize oneself as a man [*le droit à se reconnaître soi-même comme homme*]" properly belongs to this metaphysical movement of specular self-relation (R 10/30). This "*qui de droit*," as the French say "to designate a subject who has rights [*droits*]," attributes to himself the power to enact or accord some right [*droit*] or law [*droit*] (R xi/9). The Western liberal subject then is fueled by this phantasm of narcissism and imagines that it is he alone who gives himself the law and, as such, is sovereignly self-determined. And, if this sovereign self must share the polis with others, if some "living together" must take place, then it must be with "'a like, a compeer [*semblable*],' 'someone similar or semblable as a human being'" (R 11/31). Hence, the legacy of the rights of man is inexorably bound up with "the ipseity of the One, the *autos* of autonomy, symmetry, homogeneity, the same, the like, the semblable or the similar," and Derrida adds, "even, finally, God" (R 14/35).

If, as Derrida writes in *Specters of Marx*, the aporias of narcissism are "the explicit theme of deconstruction" (a point to which we will return in Part III, "Derrida: The Mourning of Narcissus"), then Derrida's corpus, from his early to his later texts, seems to devote itself to deflating any and all phantasms of narcissism and the *autos* that benefits from them rather than to rehabilitating this concept.[15] What Derrida's thought calls for, we believe, is the coupling of the deconstruction of every narcissism of the One with the reconfiguring of a narcissism, and the "right" to it, that is more open to the other *as* other.

If we now feel even more perplexed by our opening epigraph from *The Right of Inspection*, perhaps placing the epigraph within the full citation may help to clarify matters. In that text, Derrida declares:

One will never have understood anything about the love of the other, of you, of the other as such, you understand, without a new thinking of narcissism, a new "patience," a new passion for narcissism. The right to narcissism must be rehabilitated, it needs the time and the means. More narcissism, no more narcissism. [*Plus de narcissisme.*] Always more narcissism, never any more narcissism [*Toujours plus de narcissisme*]—clearly understood, including that of the other.[16] (RI XXVIII).

In the above three critiques of "the right to narcissism," we saw narcissisms that know nothing of the other, and hence all love, friendship, and hospitality are foreign to them. If Derrida, like Rousseau and Kristeva, is appealing for a new thinking of and new patience for narcissism, it is on the basis that it includes the other—both the other's narcissism and the other as the condition for the (im-)possibility of my own narcissism.

It is this latter point that the book's three parts, "Rousseau: The Passions of Narcissus," "Kristeva: The Rebirth of Narcissus," and "Derrida: The Mourning of Narcissus," will try to demonstrate.[17] In other words, by arguing that the other conditions *and* limits my self-relation and self-love, even my self-constitution, the traditional notion of narcissism (which is bound up with Ovid's influential myth of Narcissus and Echo, as well as with the Platonic distinction between being and seeming) undergoes a veritable metamorphosis, in which the love of self and love of the other can no longer be thought of as mutually exclusive but must be understood as inextricably intertwined.

Each of the above three thinkers identifies a particular "experience" in which the relation to the other is fundamental to the formation of the *self* and its narcissism, while at the same time interrupts the self's return to itself and hence, by thwarting a certain auto-affection, opens up the possibility of a relation to the other. Rousseau locates this in the experience of *pitié* (which ought to be thought of as empathy in the strongest sense, to the point of substitution); Kristeva imagines this experience to occur within "transference love" (which is not limited to the analytic scene; rather this "mystical metamorphosis" occurs in all forms of love); and Derrida locates this experience within the context of an interminable mourning (which is both structural and singular). One might say that what each is attempting to describe is im-possible—the *im-possible experience* of narcissism. Upsetting the strict division between the possible and impossible that pervades the Western philosophical tradition, Derrida defines the *im-possible* as that which is "not merely the opposite of the possible" but is "also the condition or chance of the possible."[18] If "the im-possible is everything but impossible" and if "it calls for another reflection on what possible" might mean, then narcissism, as an experience of the im-possible, would demand that one reassess all its conditions of im-possibility. One must then reconceive of the relationship between "self" and "other" out of a thinking of *an im-possible experience of narcissism.* With Rousseau, Kristeva, and Derrida, this work begins to give voice to other narratives for narcissism; that is, narcissisms that are unthinkable and unlivable without the other.

PART I

Rousseau: The Passions of Narcissus

INTRODUCTION: ANOTHER MORALITY TALE?

L'amour-propre est plus habile que le plus habile homme du monde.

  —La Rochefoucauld, *Réflexions ou sentences et maximes morales*

In the hands of the French moralists of the seventeenth century, Ovid's Narcissus does not appear as a hubristic and deluded figure but rather as a cunning and perverse passion that can outwit the most reasonable of men.[1] From Madame de Sablé's *Maximes* to Pascal's *Pensées,* the *mot du jour* of the moralists was most certainly *amour-propre,* which translated the Latin *amor sui.* As inheritors of the texts of the Church Fathers, the moralists appropriated the Augustinian opposition between *amor sui (amour-propre)* and *amor Dei (charité).*[2] In the reflections of the moralists, especially in the writings of its most famous spokesman, La Rochefoucauld, *amour-propre* appears as an unequivocally maleficent passion that must be constantly guarded against. *Amour-propre,* in La Rochefoucauld's *Réflexions ou sentences et maximes morales,* was so pervasively discussed and denounced that Voltaire in *Le Siècle de Louis XIV* wrote: *"Quoiqu'il n'y ait presque qu'une vérité dans ce livre, qui est que* l'amour-propre est le mobile de tout."[3]

As a child of the eighteenth century, Rousseau was the recipient of a rich and heavy-handed moralist tradition in which the nature and effects of self-love as *amour-propre* had been well established. Thus, it is not surprising that the young Rousseau, in one of his earliest literary ventures, authored a play, essentially a morality tale, entitled *Narcissus, or the Lover of Himself.*[4] The only play of Rousseau's to be performed publicly— for a mere two nights—has never been described as a sophisticated or significant work of theatrical literature. Even Paul de Man, one of the play's most subtle and generous readers, describes the drama thus: "To a large extent, *Narcisse* exploits the hackneyed comical resources of vanity."[5] This early work in which *amour-propre* is lightheartedly shown to make a mockery of man, a theme that is continued more critically and forcefully in Rousseau's major theoretical writings, appears to confirm that he remains faithful to the French moral tradition's condemnation of self-love as vain deceit.

Yet, as his readers are well aware, the mature Rousseau deviates from this tradition by refusing to unambiguously condemn self-love as unnatural and harmful to man.[6] Rather Rousseau, who becomes the most renowned defender of the passions, resists the moral and theoretical simplicity of his predecessors and makes an unconventional case, like that of Aristotle in the *Nicomachean Ethics*, by arguing that self-love can and should serve man's well-being.[7] In Part I, "Rousseau: The Passions of Narcissus," we undertake to show that Rousseau's deep and careful consideration of self-love—at two levels—moves away from, although never wholly breaks with, the moralists. In the first chapter, "Man's Double Birth," we examine how Rousseau, in a first move, overtly and quite polemically argues for a natural and, hence, healthy notion of self-love that he opposes to a social and malignant form. In Chapter 2, "Regarding Self-Love Anew," we make the case that Rousseau, perhaps in a less explicit yet no less powerful fashion, undermines the rigorous opposition between a purely good and an entirely evil expression of self-love that he himself had set up. It will be our contention that at this second level of analysis Rousseau, turning even further away from the intellectual naïveté of his predecessors, offers his readers a very complex and historically unprecedented version of self-love, or narcissism.

With the publication, in 1775, of the *Discourse on the Origin of Inequality*, perhaps his most famous morality tale, Rousseau introduces not one but two distinct types of self-love: *amour-propre* and *amour de soi*.[8] In apparent agreement with the tradition, he continues to relegate *amour-propre* to the place that it had held in French letters by aligning it with "errors of the imagination," in particular, with vanity or pride.[9] Nonetheless, in a radical departure from the universal condemnation of self-love, Rousseau makes the case that man's true self-love, which he terms *amour de soi*, has become, like the statue of Glaucus, disfigured and nearly unrecognizable because of the pernicious influences of society. In a return to a hypothetical state of nature, Rousseau attempts "to disentangle what is original from what is artificial in man's present Nature" and, in so doing, discovers that the human animal is animated by an instinctual self-love that makes him intensely interested in his own preservation and well-being (SD 130/OC III:123). In fact, *amour de soi* is, on Rousseau's account, the earliest operation of the human soul and, as such, is the well-spring for all others. He elaborates:

> The source of our passions, the origin and the principle of all the others, the only one born with man and which never leaves him so long as he lives is *amour de soi*—a primitive, innate passion, which is anterior to every other and of which all others are in a sense only modifications.[10]

In order to defend man's natural right to self-love, Rousseau, especially in the *Second Discourse*, engages in a polemic against the corrupting effects of civilization on man's natural condition. In this schema, *amour-propre* appears as a relative, rather than an essential, passion that perverts and supplants man's original love of himself. When depicting *amour-propre*, Rousseau often describes man's condition in pathological terms, his passions are characterized as inflamed and feverish. As opposed to *amour de soi*, which allows man to remain *within* himself, *amour-propre* causes man to be perpetually ill at ease, since he is continually comparing himself with others and, thus, is forever *outside* himself. Due to a lifetime of fomented *amour-propre*, Rousseau believes, that social man, like Glaucus's statue, is transformed and has become alien and unrecognizable, even to himself. Therefore, in this first elaboration of the conception of self-love, Rousseau establishes a stark opposition in which these "two very different passions in their nature and their effects, must not be confused" (SD 226/OC III:219).

In what we believe to be a remarkable re-elaboration of his original schema of self-love (which largely takes place in Book IV of *Emile*), Rousseau no longer exclusively champions the place and value of a natural form of self-love but now stresses the necessity for man's self-love to take shape in the social sphere and even to be transformed into a public virtue, which benefits one's self and one's species alike. In order to bring about such a shift in his own philosophy of self-love, Rousseau must undo the rigorous opposition he had established between *amour de soi* and *amour-propre*. In the second chapter, the reader is asked to take a long detour through the notion of *pitié*, as we believe it occupies an essential place in Rousseau's rethinking of the two types of self-love.

As we take this detour through *pitié*, we will discover that *pitié* is itself a detour through which self-love must travel. Self-love—both as *amour de soi* and *amour-propre*—is simultaneously deferred and expressed, restrained and unleashed in the complex process that Rousseau calls *pitié*. Therefore, we will follow the movements of *pitié* in order to trace the transformation of self-love both at the micro-level, in terms of the structures of the self, and the macro-level, in terms of the evolution of Rousseau's thinking on the subject of self-love. In so doing, we will discover that in detailing the operations of *pitié*

Rousseau *re-marks* the notion of the imagination, which has been so often devalued in his philosophy. While continuing to maintain that the powers of the human imagination, by taking man outside of himself, are potentially hazardous to his self-regard, Rousseau recognizes that the imagination—as the threshold between the self and other—must be reckoned with. And, perhaps, in spite of his own anxieties, Rousseau, we would like to show, provides a version of *pitié* that allows the thinker not only to rework the *amour de soi/amour-propre* opposition but also to reconcile the long-standing "conflict" between love of self and love of the other.

CHAPTER I

Man's Double Birth

We are, so to speak, born twice: once to exist and once to live; once for our species and once for our sex.

—*Emile*

The preceding epigraph, drawn from the second paragraph of Book IV of *Emile*, marks a dramatic split and shift between two epochs of human existence—childhood and adulthood—which are so vastly distinct for Rousseau that they each require their own birth, maturation, and education.[1] One finds this double birth, to one's species and sex, doubly inscribed in Rousseau's work: first, in the *Discourse on the Origin of Inequality*, where the development of the human race is charted from its inception (state of nature) to its demise (society), and, second, in *Emile*, where a more or less parallel map is drawn of the birth of the individual. Each text, following a developmental or genetic schema, sketches out two separate states of being that correspond to two types of dependencies. Unequivocally, Rousseau declares that "[t]here are two sorts of [human] dependence: dependence on things, which is from nature; dependence on men, which is from society" (E 85/OC IV:311). We will see that each epoch of man's existence, with its particular type of dependence, will be guided by a particular form of self-love—*amour de soi* in the case of the former and *amour-propre* in that of the latter.

THE FIRST BIRTH

Since the savage and the child are, for Rousseau, in their "natural state," their experiences are dominated by the physical, consisting of little more than sensation and need. Need, an inescapable condition of human existence, brings man in relation to and makes him dependent upon "things." In both the *Second Discourse* and *Emile*, things consist of products of nature, including the elements, plants, and animals. By emphasizing man's dependence on things rather than persons, it would seem that Rousseau is suggesting that the savage and the child exist entirely alone, cut off from all human contact.

Although Rousseau generally portrays primitive men and children as solitary beings, he does not contend that they are not involved with and reliant upon other humans. For necessity leads the savage to mate and rear children, and necessity causes the child to depend upon his mother or nurse. Rousseau insists, however, that these attachments to others are driven and sustained by pure physical need.

For example, in the state of nature, the "Physical [sentiment of love] is the general desire which moves one sex to unite with the other" (SD 164/OC III:157). However, this link between the "erotic" couple in the state of nature dissolves as soon as the flame of sexual desire is extinguished. Even the mother-child bond in the state of nature obeys the law of necessity and thus ends with the satiation of their mutual needs. Without pathos, Rousseau writes:

> The mother at first nursed her Children because of her own need; then habit made them dear to her, she nourished them because of theirs; as soon as they had the strength to forage on their own, they left even the Mother [. . .], they soon were at the point of not even recognizing each other. (SD 153/OC III:147)

Likewise, there are many instances in *Emile* when Rousseau emphasizes that the child's attachment to those who aid and care for him cannot properly be called "love" and must be understood as mere inclination toward that which meets his needs. Perhaps, none is as starkly unsentimental as the following passage from Book IV: "The child raised according to his age is alone. He knows no other attachment other than those of habit. He loves his sister as he loves his watch, and friend as his dog [. . .] Man and woman are equally alien to him" (E 219/OC IV:500). Therefore, the young Emile, Rousseau's famous fictitious charge, only knows the world in terms of its physical laws—of cause and effect, need and fulfillment—and is ignorant of the emotional and moral complexity of human existence.[2]

Then one could say that since Rousseau's savage and child are blind to and incapable of love (as well as a myriad of other passions) their relations with other humans differ little from their encounters with things. And insofar as other humans function as "things," there is no "morality" at play—no desire or dominion, no virtue or vice. Or, as Rousseau puts it in the *Second Discourse*,

> It would at first seem that men in that state, having neither moral relations of any sort [*aucune sorte de relation morale*] between them, nor known duties, could be neither good nor wicked, and had neither vices nor virtues, unless these words are taken in a physical sense and the qualities that can harm an individual's self-preservation [*sa propre conservation*] are called vices, and those that can contribute to it, virtues. (SD159/OC III:152)

As long as man's "sensibility remains limited to his own individuality," as long as he "lives in himself [*vit en lui-même*]" (SD 199/OC III:193) and his dependence is restricted to "things" (as we have defined the term), "there is nothing moral in his actions" (E 219/OC IV:501). Of course, Rousseau is not claiming that man in his natural condition is immoral but rather that he is premoral, that is to say, that he lives untouched by the influence of social relations proper and is therefore unaware of conceptions of good or evil.[3] It is important to note that Rousseau is employing the term "moral" in both a conventional (standards that govern judgment and conduct) and less conventional (social interrelations that involve recognition, obligation, power, rank, etc.) manner.[4]

If, as Rousseau suggests, we understand the terms "virtue" and "vice" in a physical sense, then whatever preserves or contributes to the preservation of man's well-being is "good" and whatever threatens or harms it is "evil."[5] Since primitive man's central concern is his self-preservation, his "love of well-being [*l'amour de bien-être*] is the sole spring of human actions" (SD 172/OC III:166). Rousseau, therefore, contends that man must love himself if he is to preserve himself and that nature must have equipped him with a keen interest in, even a passion for, his own well-being. Then, along with the first birth (to the species) and the first dependence (on things), the most primordial of all the passions is born, that is, *amour de soi*, which, according to Rousseau, "is a natural sentiment which inclines every animal to attend to its self-preservation" and which animates all of man's behavior in this epoch of his existence (SD 227/OC III:219).

THE SECOND BIRTH

Although Rousseau's primitive man may love himself, his heart is alone. He exists and is free, but he does not yet live. It is only with the second birth, with the awakening to his sex, that man truly enters into the domain of the social in which "nothing human is foreign to him" (E 212/OC IV:490). One discovers that in both the *Second Discourse* and *Emile*, it is with the dawning of sexual desire (beyond instinct) and the appearance of love that a new beginning in human life is inaugurated. Of all "the passions that stir man's heart," Rousseau declares, there is but one that "makes one sex necessary to the other" (SD 163/OC III:157). In Part II of the *Second Discourse*, he describes how the first flames of desire were ignited and sentiments of love aroused:

> The first developments of the heart were the effect of a new situation that brought Husbands and Wives, Fathers and Children to-

gether in a common dwelling; the habit of living together gave rise
to the sweetest sentiments [*les plus doux sentiments*] known to man,
conjugal love and Paternal love. (SD173–4/OC III:168)

As humans began to live and work in communal settings,
they enjoyed a newfound leisure. Rousseau imagines a festive
scene in which these idle men and women would congregate,
perhaps around a tall tree or in front of their huts, to sing and
dance. This scene is, for Rousseau, truly social—not simply
because there is a quantitative change in which greater num-
bers of humans exist in close proximity to one another, but,
more importantly, because there is a dramatic qualitative change
in rapport between them, when the "eye becomes animated
and looks over other beings" (E 220/OC IV:502).

While singing and dancing, "everyone began to look at
everyone else and to wish to be looked at himself [*Chacun com-
mença à regarder les autres et à vouloir être regardé soi-même*],
and public esteem acquired a value" (SD 175/OC III:169). As
"[o]ne begins to take an interest in those surrounding us; one
begins to feel that one is not made to live alone. It is thus that
the heart is opened to the human affections" (E 220/OC IV:502).
As if for the first time, every individual saw every other—in
relation to other members of the community and in relation to
himself. As these newly social beings grew "accustomed to attend to different objects and to make comparisons; impercepti-
bly they acquire[d] ideas of merit and of beauty which produce[d]
sentiments of preference" (SD 175/OC III:169). Thus, esteem
and privilege were accorded to the individual who seemed to
sing or dance the best, to the one who appeared the most beau-
tiful or strongest, and so forth. In this adolescence of mankind,
comparison, ranking, and preference began to dominate the
interactions between humans.

With this new organization of human relations, love is no
longer limited to an expression of animal need but emerges as a
truly human desire. Rousseau clearly distinguishes the "moral"
from the "physical" character of erotic love when he writes:

The Physical is the general desire which moves one sex to unite with
the other; the moral is what gives this desire its distinctive character
and focuses it exclusively on a single object, or at least gives it a
measure of energy for this preferred object [*cet objet préféré*]. (SD
164/OC III:157–8)

Moral, unlike physical, love cannot be satisfied with just any
individual (more accurately, with any woman, as Rousseau's
paradigmatic savage is male) and thus can only find fulfillment in a specific love object that is regarded more highly than
all the others.[6] Although he concedes that with moral love a
"tender and sweet sentiment [*un sentiment tendre et doux*] steals
into the soul," Rousseau emphasizes that "jealousy awakens
together with love" and that "the gentlest of all passions [*la plus
douce des passions*] receives sacrifices of human blood" (SD 175/
OC III:169).

In Book IV of *Emile*, Rousseau details a parallel pubescent
crisis that precipitates Emile's "second birth." Until now, the
young man, like Rousseau's savage, knew nothing of love as a
social sentiment. However, with what seems to be a furious sea-
shift, the young "man has need of a companion," and "he is no
longer an isolated being. His heart is no longer alone" (E 214/
OC IV:493). How does this remarkable transformation from a
more or less asexual child to a sexually differentiated adolescent
male occur? Not surprisingly, Rousseau, in part, attributes this
metamorphosis to the movement of nature itself. Nonetheless,
he insists, as he did in the *Second Discourse*, that even though
nature is initially responsible for sexual awakening it is only
with time and experience that we become "capable of love" (E
214/OC IV:493). He elaborates:

The inclination of instinct [*l'instinct*] is indeterminate. One sex is
attracted to another; that is the movement of nature. Choice, preferences, and personal attachments are the work of enlightenment,
prejudice, and habit. One loves only after having judged; one pre-
fers only after having compared. (E 214/OC IV:493)

Like the villagers in the *Second Discourse*, Emile's eyes are no longer silent, for they have found "a language and acquire expressiveness" and now a "nascent fire animates them" (E 212/ OC IV:490). Indeed, it is love that has quickened his glance and opened his eyes to a world of exchanged gazes. Love, for Rousseau, is never blind, "because it has better eyes than we do and sees relations we are not able to perceive" (E 214/OC IV:494). It is love that sees differences and establishes preferences; it is love that exposes Emile for the first time to the world of social ranking, with its notions of beauty and merit. "It is," therefore, "due to love that, except for the beloved object, one sex ceases to be anything for the other" (E 214/OC IV:494).

Emile not only grants preference to his ideal love object, but also, in turn, he desires to be preferred above all others. In order to obtain the preference that he accords, the young man in love must make himself more lovable than others by appearing, for example, to be the most eloquent or handsome, "at least in the eyes of the beloved object" (E 214/OC IV:494). Through love's eyes, Emile regards his peers anew and recognizes their regard for him, which inevitably leads him to compare himself with them. "And the first sentiment roused in him by this comparison," Rousseau writes, "is the desire to be in the first position [*la première place*]" (E 235/OC IV:523). Sensing how sweet it is to be loved, to be preferred, to be the most highly regarded, to be in the first position, the temptation is great to indulge the impossible desire to be loved by all, thereby unleashing inflammatory passions and with them much discontent.

Love, however, can only open man's eyes to the human realm and excite the passions because it awakens and puts in play the power of the imagination. The capacity for imagination may exist in the child and primitive man, but it is not active and thus "does not speak to [their] hearts" (SD 164/OC III:158). Once active, the imagination enables man to go outside of himself and to imagine himself in the place of others. These transports of the imagination cause the social animal to compare

his place with that of his peers. Hence, once the imagination is
ignited, "man never observes others without returning to himself and comparing himself with them," and these constant comparisons cause him to "regret being only himself" (E 243/OC
IV:535). Rousseau warns that the imagination, "which wreaks
such havoc," ultimately threatens man's self-regard (SD 164/
OC:158).

Fully in the social arena in which the highest prize is to be
(well) regarded, humans find themselves no longer primarily
dependent on things (or on persons as "things") but rather on
their fellow men. With this dependence on men, opinion sets
up "an unshakable throne" and subjects the socialized individual to the judgments of others (E 215/OC IV:494). As opposed to the savage and the child, who exist in themselves,
"sociable man, always outside himself [*hors de lui*], is capable of
living only in the opinion of others and, so to speak, derives the
sentiment of his own existence solely from their judgment"
(SD199/OC III:193). It is only when man "begins to extend outside of himself [*s'entendre hors de lui*]" that notions of good and
evil truly take hold (E 219–20/OC IV:501).[7] Therefore, unlike
dependence on things, which Rousseau argues "has no morality [and] is in no way detrimental to freedom and engenders no
vices," dependence on men begets "all the vices, and by it, master and slave are mutually corrupted" (E 85/OC IV:311).

THE PASSAGE FROM *AMOUR DE SOI* TO *AMOUR-PROPRE*

For Rousseau, it is the experience of erotic love that incites and
marks the dramatic passage from the state of nature to the social realm, from dependence on things to dependence on men.
Love, the passion that appears at the threshold between ani-
mality and humanity, is inseparable from judgment and preference, and, as such, arouses a myriad of other passions from
vanity to envy that prove fatal to innocence and happiness.[8]
This ambivalent passion is described in the *Second Discourse* as
capable of destroying what it is meant to preserve:

Among the passions that stir man's heart, there is one that is ardent, impetuous, and makes one sex necessary to the other, a terrible passion that braves all dangers, overcomes all obstacles, and in its frenzy seems liable to *destroy* Mankind when it is destined to *preserve* it. What must become of men possessed by this unbridled and brutal rage, lacking modesty, lacking restraint, and daily feuding over their loves at the cost of their blood? (SD163/OC III:157, emphasis mine)

As Derrida writes in *Of Grammatology*, "Such is the history of love [in Rousseau]. In it is reflected nothing but history as denaturalization."[9] It is thus the moral, rather than the physical, aspect of love that Rousseau portrays as a "factitious sentiment," because it thrusts man outside of himself and enslaves him to the judgmental gazes of his fellows, thereby "denaturalizing" him (SD 164/OC III:158).[10] Above all, it is man's relation to himself that is denaturalized, as his most "primitive, innate passion," *amour de soi*, is perverted and contorted into a secondary, unnatural form of self-love, which Rousseau terms *amour-propre* (E 213/OV IV:491).

The distinction between *amour de soi* and *amour-propre* is most famously and rigorously drawn in footnote XV of the *Second Discourse*, in which Rousseau unambiguously asserts:

Amour propre and *Amour de soi-même*, two very different passions in their nature and their effects, must not be confused. *Amour de soi-même* is a natural sentiment which inclines every animal to attend to its self-preservation [*veiller à sa propre conservation*] and which, guided in man by reason and modified by *pitié*, produces humanity and virtue. *Amour propre* is only a relative sentiment, factitious and born in society, which inclines every individual to set greater store by himself than by anyone else, inspires men with all the evils they do one another, and is the genuine source of honor. (SD 226/OC III:219)

Rousseau is clear in the above passage, as he is in the lines that follow it, that *amour de soi,* a wholly natural sentiment that expresses itself in all sentient creatures, ensures that man watch over "his own preservation" (E 213/OC IV:491). "And how could he watch over it if he did not take the greatest interest in it?" (E 213/OC IV:491). Only an instinctual *amour de soi*, Rousseau insists, can guarantee man's abiding interest in his preservation and well-being. Thus, he writes, "we have to love ourselves to preserve ourselves [*il faut donc que nous nous aimions pour nous conserver*]; and it follows immediately from the same sentiment that we love what preserves us [*nous aimons ce que nous conserver*]" (E 213/OC IV:492). Of course, this usage of the verb *aimer* (in both its reflexive and nonreflexive forms) operates at, what Rousseau would consider, a premoral or presocial level and is, thus, like inclination or attachment. The following passage from *Emile* demonstrates this point:

> Every child is attracted [*s'attache*] to his nurse. Romulus must have been attached [*devoit s'attacher*] to the wolf that suckled him. At first this attachment is purely mechanical [*purement machinal*]. What fosters the well-being of an individual attracts him; what harms him repels him. This is merely a blind instinct [*un instinct aveugle*]. (E 213/OC IV:492)

Thus, nature has equipped man and animal alike with *amour de soi*—"this blind inclination [*ce penchant aveugle*], devoid of any sentiment of the heart produced only a purely animal act," which operates mechanically by attaching itself to any *thing* that furthers its preservation and well-being (SD 170/OC III:164).

As previously shown, it is love proper (i.e., moral love) that turns a solitary being into a social creature and thus turns him inside out. As long as the "primitive" individual "loved nothing, he depended only on himself and his needs," in other words, he existed in and for himself (E 233/OC IV:520). But once he loves, man lives outside himself, for "[a] heart full of an overflowing sentiment likes to open itself" (E 214–15/OC IV:494). By opening his heart to others, man also opens himself up to be compared with and judged by those same others and, as a consequence, becomes "alien and ill at ease [*étranger et mal à son aise*]" when he returns to himself (E 230/OC IV:515).

If, as Rousseau suggests, all man's "relations with his species [and] all the affections of his soul are born" with love and this "first passion soon makes the others ferment," then *love of others* converts man's original self-love into its secondary and factitious form (E 214/OC IV:493). As love desires to be reciprocated, as it "wants to obtain the preference that one grants," *amour-propre* is awakened in man as a part of the movement of love itself (E 214/OC IV:494). For, if love "is the source of the first glances of one's fellows," then it "is the source of the first comparisons with them," causing man to regard himself through the eyes of another (E 214/OC IV:494). And, as we established earlier, it is comparison and the wish to be preferred that cause man to want to be in the *first position*. "This is," Rousseau writes, "the point where *amour de soi* turns into *amour-propre* and where begin to arise all the passions which depend on this one" (E 235/OC IV:523).

Since man's *amour-propre* is never content unless it is accorded first place, "the gentle and affectionate passions [. . .] born of *amour de soi*" are replaced with "the hateful and irascible passions [that] are born of *amour-propre*" (E 214/OC IV:493). In particular, when *amour de soi* no longer maintains its hold over man's heart, the inflamed passion *amour-propre* is transformed into "pride [*orgueil*] in great souls, vanity [*vanité*] in small ones, and feeds itself constantly in all at the expense of their neighbors" (E 215/OC IV:494). This relative sentiment, which "inclines every individual to set greater store by himself than by anyone else, inspires men with all the evils they do one another" (SD 226/OC III:219). In fact, the list of vices, including jealously, emulation, and enmity, that Rousseau attributes to man's *amour-propre* is quite long.

It is necessary to return once again to footnote XV in the *Second Discourse* to clarify why Rousseau believes that it is impossible for *amour-propre* to emerge in the state of nature.

Without equivocation, he declares: "I say that in our primitive state, in the genuine state of nature, *Amour-propre* does not exist" (SD 226/OC III:219). Rousseau justifies his claim that man in his natural state is uncontaminated by *amour-propre* by arguing the following:

> For, since every individual human being views himself as the *only Spectator* to observe him, as the *only being* in the universe to take any interest in him, as the *only judge* in his own merit, it is not possible that a sentiment which originates in comparisons he is not capable of making, could spring up in his soul. (SD 226–27/OC III:219, emphasis mine)

Without the ability—although he possesses the capacity—to perceive position and rank among humans, man in his "primitive state" (a state in which the child must analogously be included) cannot reflect on his own position vis-à-vis others. As Rousseau repeatedly emphasizes, the savage and the child are "alone" (i.e., without human or "moral" relations) in the world and as such cannot make comparisons. Thus primitive man, protected from the opinions and judgments of others, is alone his own spectator and his sole judge (an important point to which we will return). In both texts discussed, especially *The Discourse on the Origin of Inequality*, Rousseau warns that when man develops a distance from himself and finds himself outside himself, he is at risk of losing his original *amour de soi*, which causes him to vigilantly watch over his well-being. Therefore, as long as man remains alone with himself, in other words, *within* himself, nothing from *outside* man can divert or damage his *amour de soi*. It would be reasonable to conclude from what we have seen that *amour-propre* is as alien to the savage and the child as are other men. And, by the same logic, we can safely say that if *amour-propre* is awakened in man, he is no longer in his natural state.

In our reading thus far we have followed, for the most part, the contours of the conventionally accepted interpretation of the two forms of self-love in Rousseau and have traced the role that each passion plays in man's "double birth." This binary and often naïve narrative, which depicts *amour de soi* as natural and benign and *amour-propre* as the unnatural, thus malignant, substitute for the former, is clearly not the invention of Rousseau's readers and commentators.[11] Indeed, as we have tried to demonstrate with his own words, this history of man's denaturalization at both the individual and social levels is most certainly Rousseau's. Yet, Rousseau's texts, in particular *Emile*, are hardly consistent or unambiguous on the meaning and function of these two passions. Although we harbor no desire to save "Rousseau" as such or to claim that the above reading of his texts is misguided, we would like to argue in the remainder of Part I that his thinking about self-love, indebted as it is to the moralists who preceded him, offers a more complex logic of self-relation that twists away from the positions of his predecessors.

CHAPTER 2

Regarding Self-Love Anew

I would find someone who wanted to prevent the birth of the passions almost as mad as someone who wanted to annihilate them.
    —*Emile*

The neat parallelism and apparent continuity between the *Second Discourse* and *Emile* begins to break down if one examines these two texts more carefully. Perhaps some of the conflation of the ideas in these two works is because *Emile*, a text primarily relegated to pedagogical studies in the English-speaking world, is little or poorly read in the discipline of philosophy. Yet, the most extensive and nuanced treatment of the two forms of self-love in Rousseau's corpus is found in *Emile*. One Anglophone scholar, Nicholas Dent, who has devoted serious attention to the notions of *amour de soi* and *amour-propre* in Rousseau's writings claims that

> the first forty or so pages of Book IV of *Emile*, in which Rousseau intensively addresses the issues under consideration here, are among the most dense and intricate in the whole work, and deserve, and would reward, the same closeness of discussion as is granted as a matter of course to, say, a few lines of Aristotle or Kant.[1]

Let us, then, turn our attention to a number of these "dense and intricate" passages to show how Rousseau reformulates and thus complicates the more-or-less oppositional schema developed in the *Second Discourse.*[2]

As in his earlier work, Rousseau maintains in *Emile* that *amour de soi* is the source of all of man's passions—"the origin and the principle of all the others, the only one born with man and which never leaves him so long as he lives" (E 212–13/OC IV:491). And this primal passion, which is "anterior to every other," remains active within man throughout the course of his life (E 213/OC IV:491). However, this "first" and wholly natural passion must express itself within the context of man's encounters with the world. Therefore, external influences or (what Rousseau calls) "alien causes [*des causes étrangéres*]" modify the original passion and its purpose (E 213/OC IV:491). Although the source is natural and, by extension, "all passions are natural," Rousseau worries that these modifications are potentially hazardous to man's preservation and well-being—the proper ends of *amour de soi* (E 213/OC IV:491). "All those [passions] which subject us and destroy us," Rousseau declares, "come from elsewhere [*viennent d'ailleurs*]" (E 212/OC IV:491). Further, he insists that "countless alien streams [*mille ruisseaux étrangers*] have swollen [the original source]. It is a great river which constantly grows and in which one could hardly find a few drops of its first waters" (E 212/OC IV:491). Thus, Rousseau contends that when "man finds himself *outside* of nature [*l'homme se trouve hors de la nature*]" he will exist in "contradiction with himself" (E 213/OC IV:491, emphasis mine).

Nonetheless, in the same book of *Emile*, Rousseau concedes that "[t]hese dangerous passions will, I am told, be born sooner or later in spite of us. I do not deny it" (E 226/OC IV:510). With trepidation, but without fatalism, he accepts that *amour-propre* and related passions will be born in man. In fact, as cited in the epigraph to this chapter, Rousseau unequivocally asserts that his aim has never been to prevent or suppress the birth of the passions. In the same passage, Rousseau, speaking directly to his readers, offers a word of caution: "Those who believed that this was my project up to now would surely have understood me very badly [*ceux qui croiroient que tel a été mon projet jusqu'ici m'auroient surement fort mal entendu*]" (E 212/OC IV:491). He adds that all of man's passions, not simply *amour de soi*, are "the principal instruments of [his] preservation. It is, therefore, as vain as it is ridiculous to want to destroy them—it is to control nature, it is to reform the work of God" (E 212/OC IV:490–91).

In claiming both that the *only* truly natural passion, uncontaminated by all alien influences, is *amour de soi* and that *all* passions are divine and natural, thus instruments of man's self-preservation, Rousseau seems to be caught in an absurd contradiction. Without trying to paper over the tensions in his text or attempting to propose a logical resolution to this paradox, we would like to suggest a way of approaching the problem. If we were to take Rousseau at his word when he writes in the preface to the *Second Discourse* that "it is no light undertaking to disentangle what is original from what is artificial in man's present Nature" and that, in truth, it is not possible "to know accurately a state [man's natural state] which no longer exists, which perhaps never did exist, which probably will never exist," then we would be forced to reconsider the relationship between *amour de soi* and *amour-propre* (SD 130/OC III:124). Such a reconsideration would open up a number of critical and difficult questions: Are these two passions both proper to the human being and, hence, equally necessary for his well-being? If *amour-propre* is indeed proper to man, is it still an "unnatural" and wholly perverse passion? And, perhaps most important, are *amour de soi* and *amour-propre* truly two separate passions or "two names for the same divided passion"?[3] However, before we can attend to these questions, it is necessary to take a detour through Rousseau's notion of *pitié*.

PITIÉ: MAN OUTSIDE HIMSELF

Pitié, although natural to man's heart, would remain forever inactive without imagination to set it in motion. How do we let ourselves be moved to pity? By transporting ourselves outside ourselves; by identifying with the suffering being?

—*Essay on the Origin of Languages*

In the *Second Discourse*, Rousseau cites not one but two fundamental "operations of the human soul" that precede the activity of the imagination and the functioning of reason (SD 132/
OC III:125). The first, *amour de soi*, as we have witnessed in previous sections, "interests us intensely in our well-being and
our self-preservation" and the second, *pitié*, "inspires in us a
natural repugnance at seeing any sentient Being, and especially
any being like ourselves, perish or suffer" (SD 132/OC III:126).
Pitié, according to Rousseau, is both a disposition suitable to
creatures that are weak and suffer and a practical virtue that
"precedes the exercise of all reflection" (SD 160/OC III:154).
Nature, then, has not only armed man with an instinctual self-
love that guides him, independent of reason, to preserve his
well-being, but it has also equipped him with a natural aversion to and sympathy for the suffering of other sentient beings.
(It is important, as will become clear, to note that in the *Second
Discourse* Rousseau extends these natural operations of the soul,
in particular *pitié*, to man and animal alike.)[4]

At first, it appears that these two activities of the human
soul are for Rousseau equally primordial. Yet, upon closer inspection, one finds that *pitié*, in fact, derives from *amour de soi*
and, thus, is "the first relative sentiment which touches the human heart" (E 222/OC IV:504). In *Emile*, Rousseau depicts the
concern for and love of one's fellows as an outgrowth of man's
originary *amour de soi*: "A child's first sentiment is to love himself [*s'aimer lui-même*]; and the second, which derives from the
first [*qui dérive du prémier*], is to love those who come near
him" (E 213/OC IV:492). Later, in the same chapter, he adds:
"Love of men derived from love of self [*L'amour des hommes
dérivé de l'amour de soi*] is the principle of human justice" (E
235/OC IV:523). The name of this principle of justice, which
transforms the love of self into the love of others, is none other
than *pitié*.

Pitié, in Rousseau's estimation, is virtuous and just, because in
diverting and thereby moderating "in every individual the activity of *amour de soi* [it] contributes to the mutual preservation [*la
conservation mutuelle*] of the entire species" (SD 162/OC III:156).[5]

In another passage, Rousseau asserts that *pitié* limits self-love in both of its forms: It "soften[s] the ferociousness of his *amour-propre* (XV), or the desire for self-preservation before the birth of this love, tempering his ardor for well-being with an innate repugnance to see his kind [*son semblable*] suffer" (SD160/OC III:154).[6] *Pitié*, therefore, does not simply limit the vain excesses of *amour-propre* but also deters man from being wholly concerned with his own preservation and well-being. If *pitié* restrains the force of self-love, it does so, we would like to suggest, "less by opposing itself to it than by expressing it in an indirect way, by deferring it" (OG 175/248). This diversion is, as Derrida argues in *Of Grammatology*, "less an estrangement and an interruption of the love of self [*l'amour de soi*] than its first and most necessary consequence" (OG 174/248).

We must pause to consider how self-love, which is fundamentally self-referential, is indirectly expressed as *pitié* and thus channeled toward others. In the *Essay on the Origin of Languages*, Rousseau argues that although *pitié* is natural to the human animal, it "would remain forever inactive without imagination to set it in motion."[7] In apparent opposition to his position in the *Second Discourse*, in which he claims that *pitié*, like *amour de soi*, precedes all operations of the imagination and all processes of reflection, Rousseau maintains in both the *Essay* and *Emile* that *pitié* is only possible in so far as the imagination has been awakened. "[N]o one," Rousseau writes, "becomes sensitive until his imagination is animated" (E 223/OC IV:505–6), because it is only by way of the imagination that we "feel the ills of others" (E 231/OC IV:517).

It is necessary, then, to ask how exactly does the imagination facilitate compassion and sympathy and by what mechanisms does the imagination allow man to be moved by *pitié*. In the *Essay*, Rousseau argues that it is "by transporting ourselves outside ourselves [*en transportant hors de nous-mêmes*]; by identifying with the suffering being [*en nous identifiant avec l'être souffrant*]" that we become capable of *pitié* (EOL 261/OC V:395).[8] Interestingly, in *Emile*, Rousseau employs nearly the exact words and phrasing to describe the process of *pitié*:

> In fact, how do we let ourselves be moved by pity if not by trans-porting ourselves outside of ourselves [*en nous transportant hors de nous*] and identifying with the suffering animal [*en nous indentifi-ant avec l'animal souffrant*], by leaving, as it were, our own being to take on its being [*en quittant pour ainsi dire notre être pour prendre le sien*]? (E 223/OC IV 505–6)

The imagination thus has the power to transport us out of our-selves, beyond the limits of our own experiences, and enables us not only to go beyond our own being but also to take on the being of another by identifying with his sufferings. For the sake of our analysis, let us logically separate these two elements of *pitié*—being *transported outside* one's self and *identifying with* the other's pain—that are experientially simultaneous.

Although Rousseau consistently claims that the imagination is what forces man out of the immanence of his being, in which his own sensations and sentiments alone have reality, he depicts the consequences of being transported outside oneself in starkly divergent ways. As we saw in Chapter 1, Rousseau, primarily in the *Second Discourse*, gives a distinctly different inflection to man's being "outside of himself [*hors de lui*]" than we find in his portrayal of *pitié* above. We should recall that Rousseau had asserted that man, in his natural state, "lives in himself [*vit en lui-même*]," as his imagination is dormant (SD 199/OC III:193). And, it is only when the passion of love is aroused that the imagi-nation is ignited, causing man to find himself everywhere but in himself. From the newborn desire to be loved and preferred, "sociable man, always outside of himself [*hors de lui*]," becomes dependent upon and lives off of the opinions and judgments of others (SD 199/OC III:193). In this schema, for man to be out-side of himself is nothing less than for him to lose himself, to become a stranger to himself, that is to say, to cease being a man.

Yet, in *Emile*, Rousseau contends that for man to become fully human he must not remain alone and closed within himself. "So long as his sensibility remains limited to his own individuality, there is nothing moral in his actions. It is only when it begins to extend outside of himself [*s'étendre hors de lui*]," Rousseau declares, that he can be constituted "as a man and as an integral part of the species" (E 219–20/OC IV:501). This is because an individual "who has never reflected cannot be clement, or just, or pitying any more than he can be wicked and vindictive. He who imagines nothing feels only himself; in the midst of mankind he is alone" (EOL 261/OC V:396). Even the child's "apparent insensibility" to the ills of others "is soon changed into compassion," when, through imagination, he begins to extend beyond the empirical confines of his person.[9] Rousseau repeatedly insists in *Emile* that the "physical sentiment of our ills" is insufficient to make us compassionate and that "it is only the imagination which makes us feel the ills of others" (E 231/OC IV:517). For, through *pitié*, "it is not in ourselves, it is in him [the other] that we suffer [*c'est dans lui que nous souffrons*]" (E 223/OC IV 505–6). This transport outside of oneself in which one suffers in the place of the other—this movement that distinguishes the adult from the child, as well as the human from the animal—could be said to be "the becoming-human of *pitié*" (OG 182/262). Thus, it is only by virtue of the imagination that the human animal is able to go beyond himself and move outside the mute and solitary suffering that remains the beast's.

However, Rousseau insists in the *Second Discourse* that "Beasts themselves sometimes show evident signs" of *pitié*, which are most commonly expressed as a kind of discomfort or agitation at the sight or sound of another animal, especially one of its own kind, in distress (SD 160/OC III:154). Yet, *pitié*, as it is defined in *Emile* and the *Essay*, is precisely what distinguishes man from animal. What separates the human from the beast in the *Second Discourse* is not *pitié* but rather fear of death, "for an animal will never know what it is to die, and the knowledge of death and its terrors was one of man's first acquisitions in moving away from the animal condition" (SD 150/OC III:143).

However, if we reflect on this distinction more carefully, we find that it is man's burgeoning capacity to imagine—to transport himself beyond the present—that exposes him to the terror of death.[10] This anticipation of death, which is proper to man, is inextricably bound up with the awakening of the imagination. And, if the imagination, which exposes the human animal to the suffering and death of the other *as* other, moves man to *pitié*, then we would have to conclude that *pitié* is the becoming human of man.[11]

The other essential aspect of *pitié* is identifying with the being that suffers. Even in the *Second Discourse*, where he emphatically denies that the imagination plays any role in *pitié*, Rousseau writes that "commiseration will be all the more energetic in proportion as the onlooking animal *identifies* more intimately with the suffering animal" (SD 162/OC III:155, emphasis mine). In fact, in several places in the *Second Discourse*, Rousseau expressly says that we are particularly moved by *pitié* when we witness "any being like ourselves [*principalement nos semblables*], perish or suffer" (SD 132/OC III:126). As we recall, he claims that it is man's "innate repugnance to see his kind [*son semblable*] suffer" that tempers and modifies his self-love (SD160/OC III:154). Even though Rousseau qualifies these claims by suggesting that "this identification must, clearly, have been infinitely closer in the state of Nature than in the state of reasoning," it seems undeniable that the imagination, however primitive or rudimentary, must be functioning for "primitive man" to judge his similarity or likeness to another and hence to be moved by *pitié* (SD 162/OC III:156).

(It is necessary at this juncture to open up a brief parenthesis regarding the imagination in the state of nature. In terms of his rhetoric, Rousseau refuses to admit that a being in his natural state is capable of imagining or reflecting. In a polemical tone, he writes: "I almost dare assert, the state of reflection is a state against Nature, and the man who meditates a depraved animal" [SD 145/OC III:138]. Yet, as has been shown above, the operations of *pitié* require that the onlooker identifies, no matter how tenuously, with the suffering being. Thus, in order to experience empathy, the savage must not only observe other beings but also be capable of comparing them with his own existence. Therefore, despite his declarations to the contrary, Rousseau's own argument presupposes that "natural man" is not entirely enclosed within immanence but is already at a distance from himself by virtue of the workings of the imagination. In *Allegories of Reading*, Paul de Man makes the case that within "the fictional state of nature" Rousseau inscribes a "specular, reflective distance" at the heart of man's relationship to himself [DM 165]. As evidence he cites the following passage from the *Second Discourse*: "Every individual human being views himself [*se regardant lui-même*] as the only Spectator to observe him, as the only being in the universe to take any interest in him, as the only judge in his own merit" [SD 226–27/ OC III 19]. As de Man points out, even within the hypothetical state of nature, man, as his own spectator and judge, is already at a distance from himself, outside of himself, and reflecting upon himself, however crude or elementary these operations may be.)

To be transported to the place of the other and to suffer in his place requires, according to Rousseau, similitude. In the *Essay*, he asks: "How could I suffer when I see another suffer, if I do not even know that he suffers, if I do not know what he and I have in common?" (EOL 261/OC V:395). In order to become sensitive to the ills of others and capable of compassion, man, in his primitive state (as a youth or in the childhood of mankind) must first become aware "that there are beings like him [*qu'il y a des êtres semblables*] who suffer what he has suffered, who feel the pains he has felt, and that there are others whom we ought to conceive of as able to feel them too" (E 222/ OC IV:504). For Rousseau, then, the abyss between the self and other must be bridged by the imagination, which allows the self to discover itself in another, but not just in any other, in its fellow, "*dans son semblable.*"

Therefore, if identification with one's kind is essential to *pitié*, Rousseau, the pedagogue, suggests that Emile's imagination should be aroused by "teach[ing] him that he has fellows [*des semblables*]" (E 220/OC IV:502). And, his "fellows" would at first be those who are most proximate to him, "whom habit has made dear and necessary to him" and "whose nature has a more manifest identity with his own" (E 233/OC IV:520). This "manifest identity," of which Rousseau speaks, seems to be less a cultural or ethnic semblance and more a reflection of shared sufferings among finite beings. What binds a human being to those around him is less their pleasures than their pains, since "we see far better in the latter the identity of our natures with theirs and the guarantees of their attachment to us. If our common needs unite us by interest," Rousseau declares, "our common miseries unite us by affection" (E 221/OC IV:503).[12]

In *Emile*, he then suggests that for a youth to become truly humane his imagination must be unsettled and extended by exposing him to "the vicissitudes of fortune" and making him aware that he, as a finite being, is not exempt from these unhappy fates (E 224/OC IV:508). Rousseau prescribes this education for his Emile because, as he asserts in the "Second Maxim" of *pitié*, one "pities in others those ills from which one does not feel oneself exempt"; that is to say, one is moved to *pitié* in so far as one imagines that he is *like* others (E 224/OC IV:507). If what defines the human condition is frailty and finitude, as "all are subject to the miseries of life, to sorrows, ills, needs, and pains of every kind" and, in the end, "all are condemned to death," then one's fellow must be each and every mortal (E 221/ OC IV:503). Yet, a youth, as Rousseau points out, will not immediately identify with all men and the word "mankind" will not initially signify anything to him. The abstract idea of humanity is insufficient to move Emile to *pitié*. Rather, he will come to identify with "his species [*son espèce*]" (E 233/OC IV:520) if, and only if, "he finds himself in all [*il se retrouve dans toutes*]" (E 226/OC IV:510).[13]

Let us return to the question of self-love, that is, if we ever really strayed too far from it. When we embarked on our detour through *pitié*, we discovered that *pitié* is itself a detour that defers and interrupts the self-love from which it is derived. We also found that *pitié* modifies and thereby limits the expression of self-love in both its forms: "the ferociousness of [. . .] *amour-propre*" and the "ardor for well-being"; that is, *amour de soi* (SD160/OC III:154). We also suggested, but did not substantiate, that in deferring the direct expression of either *amour de soi* or *amour-propre* that *pitié* is an indirect manifestation of self-love. In a detailed footnote in Book IV of *Emile*, Rousseau teases out the moment during *pitié* in which the self, in identifying with its fellow, is no longer in itself but suffers in his fellow, *as* his fellow. Right at the core of *pitié*—in the midst of this intense identification—Rousseau locates the workings of self-love. He writes that when

> I feel that I am, so to speak, in him, it is in order not to suffer that I do not want him to suffer. I am interested in him for love of myself [*je m'interesse à lui pour l'amour de moi*], and the reason for the precept is in nature itself, which inspires in me the desire of my well-being in whatever place I feel my existence [*qui m'inspire le désir de mon bien-être en quelque lieu que je me sente éxister*]. (E 235/OC IV:523)

Pitié, thus, not only prevents man from turning back on himself and devoting himself solely to his own well-being, but also, perhaps through a ruse of "nature," it mobilizes man's love of self, which always desires its well-being in whatever place it feels itself, for the well-being of the other. This transport of self-love through the complex movements of *pitié*, then, clarifies Rousseau's claim that love of other is derived from love of self. And, this is, in his estimation, not a cause for shame or disappointment, as man's self-love is neither sin nor folly but plays a much nobler role in human existence: "Love of men derived from *amour de soi*," Rousseau proclaims, is nothing less than the "the principle of human justice" (E 235/ OC IV:523).

THE VIRTUE OF *AMOUR-PROPRE*

I have difficulty believing that someone who loves only himself can disguise himself well enough to be as pleasing as someone who draws from his attachment to others a new sentiment of happiness.

—*Emile*

Our examination of *pitié* reveals that the logic at work in the *Second Discourse*, which upheld the polarity between *amour de soi* and *amour-propre*, has shifted in *Emile*. *Amour de soi*, which throughout Rousseau's writings consistently names the desire or instinct for well-being, was aligned with the figure of the solitary savage, who, deprived of an active imagination, existed in and for himself. *Amour-propre*, a much more charged term in Rousseau's corpus, which designates in the most minimal sense the activity of "the relative I [*le moi relative*]," appeared to cause social man to exist at an uncomfortable distance from himself (E 243/OC IV:534). A certain reading of Rousseau would conclude, then, that for man to be truly happy he must live a solitary existence and love only himself (in terms of *amour de soi*), lest he expose himself to the unhappiness that relations with his peers, by awakening in him vain self-regard (i.e., *amour-propre*), could cause. Although it is true that on numerous occasions Rousseau displays anxiety about man's dependence on others and the potential harmful effects it may have on man's self-relation, he also asserts: "I do not conceive how someone who needs nothing can love anything. I do not conceive how someone who loves nothing can be happy" (E 221/ OC IV:503). Rousseau, the thinker who so persuasively argues that man has a (natural) right, thus a fundamental obligation, to love himself—to care for his well-being and to ensure a healthy self-regard—equally contends that a man who loves himself alone will be neither pleasing to others nor happy.

We have seen that it is Rousseau's notion of *pitié* that, in simultaneously limiting and expressing self-love, reconciles the dual demand to love oneself and to love others. Moreover, it is through the elaboration of the structures of *pitié* that Rousseau undoes the supposed conflict between *amour de soi* and *amour-propre* by reinscribing the function and value of the imagination, as well as the exteriority it opens up. Being outside oneself, existing in and as the other, is not only put forward as part of his descriptive or structural account of *pitié* but also is offered by Rousseau as a prescriptive; that is, as a better way to negotiate the self and/as other relation. In order to justify this claim, we must recall that the inflammatory activity of the imagination and the alienating experience of "being outside oneself [*hors de soi*]" was most intimately associated with the workings of *amour-propre*. Yet, in his detailed and considered analysis of *pitié*, it is the imagination (as exteriority and identification) that opens the solipsistic savage and child to the other, to all others, and, with that opening, to the possibility of friendship, love, and happiness.

Rousseau goes so far as to prescribe that a tutor should provide his pupil with numerous opportunities to go beyond himself through *pitié*. Rather than confining the youth's heart in the insular world of pure *amour de soi* (as if such a state were possible), he suggests to the educator:

> To excite and nourish the nascent sensibility, to guide it or follow it in its natural inclination, what is there to do other than to offer the young man objects on which the expansive force of his heart can act—objects which swell the heart [*qui le dilatent*], which extend it to other beings [*qui l'étendent sur les autres êtres*], which make it find itself everywhere outside itself [*qui le fassent partout retrouver hors de lui*]—and carefully to keep away those which contract and concentrate the heart and tighten the spring of the human I? (E 223/ OC IV:506)

While Rousseau may be stressing that Emile should be exposed to certain objects rather than others (to those sights and sounds that arouse sympathy rather than those that encourage envy), what is most significant is that he insists that for Emile to truly become human his heart must be extended and expanded, via the workings of the imagination, thus *finding itself* everywhere outside itself.[14] In other words, it is only by enlarging the heart—the spring of the human *I*—that man will find himself.

Rousseau does not deny that this expansion of the *I* is without benefit or profit for the self (as well as for the other).[15] For, when one partakes in the sufferings of one's fellows, one not only takes pleasure in commiseration (the moment of identification), but also feels a certain happiness from being exempt from the other's plight (the moment of nonidentification).[16] This double pleasure, gained from identification and nonidentification, reveals how both forms of self-love are given expression through *pitié*. Through identification with another creature in pain, *amour de soi*, which attends to its well-being wherever it senses itself, is satisfied. And, in the movement away from identification with the suffering of the other, *amour-propre* is gratified, as it is content with its own position. Therefore, could one not legitimately claim that the drive for well-being animates the desire to be pleased with one's place vis-à-vis others? If we answer yes, and I believe that we must answer in the affirmative, then we must concede that the relationship between these two passions, if they are truly two separate passions, is much more interdependent than it would first appear.

By way of concluding this chapter, which traces the transformation of Rousseau's thinking of self-love, we would like to propose some speculative and suggestive remarks that, no doubt, will raise more questions than can be adequately addressed here. If, as was alluded to earlier in the chapter, we take Rousseau's "disclaimers" concerning the status of the state of nature seriously, then we could risk making the argument that *amour de soi* is a form of self-love that "no longer exists, which perhaps never did exist, which probably will never exist." In other words, *amour de soi* as such, as a passion wholly anterior to and independent of other passions, is a purely hypothetical construct, yet a necessary one that permits Rousseau to wrest self-love from the debased position that it was assigned by the moralists. Yet, if the notion of *amour de soi*—the pure and autonomous drive for one's well-being—were to survive in Rousseau's thought, ironically it would only be through *amour-propre*. Insofar as *amour-propre* is the functioning of the *I* as it is socially constituted, then the drive for well-being can only exist if it is expressed in and as *amour-propre*.

We would have to conclude that Rousseau's early unequivocal and overly moralistic condemnation of *amour-propre* is no longer tenable and, in the light of his later works, such an interpretation of this passion is no longer justifiable. As we witnessed in the last section, it is his supple and sophisticated account of *pitié* developed in *Emile* and echoed in the *Essay on the Origins of Language* that allows Rousseau to write the following words, words that are as surprising as they are remarkable: "Let us extend *amour-propre* to other beings. We shall transform it into a virtue, and there is no man's heart in which this virtue does not have its root" (E 252/OC IV:547).

PART II

Kristeva: The Rebirth of Narcissus

INTRODUCTION: SELF-LOVE—BEYOND SIN, SYMPTOMS, AND SUBLIME VALUES

Narcissus knows one cannot go beyond narcissism, but without fretting over it he builds temporary, gossamer, limpid loves [. . .]. Disenchanted, but not depressed, Narcissus no longer takes himself, since Freud, for a sin or a sublime value, but rather for that infinitely distant boundary marker on the basis of which an immediately *symbolic sensuality* [*une sensualité immédiatement symbolique*] attempts to take shape (my emphasis).
    —*Tales of Love*

In the opening line of a yet to be translated text, *L'amour de soi et ses avatars: Démesure et limites de la sublimation,* Julia Kristeva writes: "Self-love is perhaps the most enigmatic expression, and experience, there is."[1] One only needs to take a cursory look back at Western discourses, be they philosophical, religious, or literary, from Aristotle to Kant's ethical treatments of *philautia,* from Plotinus to Aquinas's more metaphysical speculations on the subject, from La Rochefoucauld to Rousseau's moral reflections on *amour de soi* and *amour-propre,* to confirm the

veracity of Kristeva's assertion.[2] Considering the scope of the
thinkers who have carefully and critically treated the thorny
question of self-love, it is simply daunting to broach the subject. But, perhaps, it is even more treacherous to raise the issue
if one intends to offer a sympathetic interpretation of this much
maligned term and experience. This is precisely what Kristeva
has had the courage to undertake in her writings from the
1980s and '90s, notably in *Tales of Love, New Maladies of the
Soul*, and *The Sense and Non-Sense of Revolt*, to her recent texts,
especially in her treatment of the life and writings of Melanie
Klein and Colette in *Female Genius: Life, Madness, Words—
Hannah Arendt, Melanie Klein, Colette*.[3]

Nonetheless, Kristeva's most extensive meditation on the
experience of self-love can still be found in her 1983 *Tales of Love*,
a text that is devoted to a study of the powerful and inextricable relationship between love of the self and love of the other in
Western letters.[4] Although Kristeva, in the introduction to this
book, promises the reader "a philosophy of love," she devotes
several chapters, including the opening chapter on Freud, to an
elaboration of self-love. In the book's first chapter, "Freud and
Love: Treatment and Its Discontent," she writes "[i]n his journey through the land of love Freud reaches Narcissus," and
throughout the book she repeatedly draws our attention to the
fact that this enigmatic experience of self-love has been framed,
since the time of Ovid, by the myth and figure of Narcissus
(TL 21/31). Therefore, in *Tales of Love*, Kristeva traces the various incarnations of this malleable and resourceful character,
because she is convinced that Narcissus has been and remains
"essential as a source of western subjectivism" (TL 115/146), and
thus insists that it is "interesting today to stress the originality
of the narcissistic figure and the entirely singular (*toute singu-
laire*) place it occupies, in the history of Western subjectivity"
(TL 105/134).[5]

In her account of the historical metamorphoses of Narcissus, Kristeva reveals that this paradigmatic figure of self-love
has represented on the one hand a fatal error or mortal sin and

on the other a sublime value. If one turns to Ovid's own portrayal of Narcissus, not to mention the Plotinian allusions to this myth in *The Enneads*, one discovers the double error of Narcissus: one epistemological, the other ethical. Narcissus is condemned not only for loving appearances instead of reality— that is, for confusing seeming with being—but also for morbidly shutting himself off from any outside, with refusing to turn toward the other, and, ultimately, with the failure to love. Kristeva also suggests that there was a countercurrent to the devaluation of self-love that found its fullest expression in Christianity and is exemplified in the writings of the Church Fathers.[6] In these writings, the narcissistic figure found salvation and was freed to love himself with abandon, insofar as he loves himself for and because of God.[7] This moral imperative to love oneself because God first loved you transformed self-love from a sin into a sublime value.

In the modern world, self-love, now translated into the language of medicine, specifically psychiatry, emerges neither as a sin nor a sublime value but instead as a symptom; in other words, as pathology. Kristeva writes: "When Freud took the word narcissism back from the realm of psychiatry, Narcissus again and more than ever caused discomfort; Narcissus had become a perverse symptom" (TL 123/155).[8] Nonetheless, the telltale "narcissistic" symptoms—including paranoia and grandiosity, melancholy and the inability to love—are perhaps nothing more than another way of configuring the original errors of Narcissus: delusion and egoism. It is, of course, not surprising that Kristeva is acutely aware of the suffering that these symptoms can cause the modern subject, because, as she notes, "[t]he analyst is by definition tuned in to the crisis [and] the analytic contract issues from the inevitable discontent" (TL 372/462).

In fact, Kristeva charges that the aforementioned symptoms expose a contemporary crisis in the capacity for love. In other words, she is suggesting that these critical, yet all too common, symptoms of the modern individual arise from an inability to find a discourse for love, or, that is, an incapacity to speak and exist within the boundaries of a lover's discourse. This failure to set up the codes and parameters of a lover's language or, more precisely, to articulate language as love, as identification, or as transference, ironically "reveals our inability to respond to narcissism" (TL 381/472). Further, Kristeva claims in *Tales of Love* that because "amatory experience rests on narcissism" (TL 267/331), "all love discourses have dealt with narcissism and have set themselves up as codes of positive, ideal values" (TL 7/16).

Ironically, in a time when there seems to be no absence of narcissistic symptoms, Kristeva asserts that what we are witness to is "our being unable today to elaborate primary narcissism" (TL 374/464). Thus, she concludes that these contemporary crises in love, or as one Kristeva commentator describes it— our modern failure "to accommodate the corporeal, affective, and mimetic dimension of separateness and connection with others"—is paradoxically not predicated on our having too much narcissism, but rather is a consequence of our not having enough.[9] Thus, for Kristeva, a new discourse about love and subjectivity would require a coming to terms with the figure of Narcissus and a re-elaboration of the psychoanalytic notion of narcissism.[10]

While being attentive to the historical specificity of subject formation and while arguing that some epochs developed discourses that gave fuller expression to the ego as affective, Kristeva claims that what psychoanalysis has revealed is "the permanency, [or] the inescapable nature of crisis"; that is to say, what is not epochal for her is that "[t]he speaking being is a wounded being, his speech wells up out of an aching for love" (TL 372/462).[11] Thus she applauds Freud for recognizing that "narcissism" is fundamentally neither a sin nor a symptom but a structure.[12] As opposed to his contemporaries, Kristeva says that "Freud used [the word 'narcissism'] in a different way in order to stress the organization which is universal for every person, which is not symptomatic, in the sense that a symptom may be considered as an illness or something pejorative, but which is universal in the organization of every psychic space."[13]

Perhaps Kristeva is overly generous to Freud when she accords him full credit for the discovery and articulation of the narcissistic structure. Readers of Freud would be well aware that the notion of narcissism is one of the most complex and unclear concepts in his corpus, with which Freud himself was never satisfied.[14] We highlight this point not to discredit Kristeva's assertion that Freud shows us that narcissism is first and foremost a structure but to give credit where credit is due. It is, we believe, the force and the creativity of Kristeva's own interpretation of Freud (no doubt in dialogue with, but also in distinction from, the work of other psychoanalytic thinkers such as Jacques Lacan, Melanie Klein, and André Green), which allows us to conceive of self-love "as a primary identity organization" that enables the emergence of a subject.[15] Therefore, the originality and radicality of Kristeva's theory of self-love, as opposed to those of her many predecessors, lies in her success in shunning the temptation to reduce narcissism to a value—be it positive or negative—and asserts that self-love is indispensable to the life of the subject as a speaking being.

In order to examine Kristeva's account of the narcissistic structure, we will, in Chapter 3, "Reconceiving Freud's Narcissus," first return to her reading of Freud's demarcation between autoeroticism and narcissism to demonstrate that although self-love is neither innate nor originary, as someone like Rousseau suggests (see Part I, "Rousseau: The Passions of Narcissus"), it is nonetheless essential for the development of the subject.[16] Further, we will show that as opposed to most conceptions of narcissism, which posit either a monadic or a fusional dyadic state, Kristeva argues that narcissism is a ternary structure that precedes the emergence of the Oedipus complex. The three terms composing the narcissistic structure include two poles, the maternal and the third party, and the emerging subject who vacillates between each. What we will be tracing in this chapter is the double movement that will create the space in which a subject can emerge. These two movements—separation and transference, one as essential as the other—form, as Sara Beardsworth writes, the "central node of connection and disconnection, fullness and emptiness, positions and losses" (SB 374) that intertwines the "semiotic," the realm of the drives, and the "symbolic," the domain of signs, and generates, what Kristeva calls, "an immediate symbolic sensuality" (TL 125/158).

In brief, the very first movement in the process of individuation in the life of the subject-to-be involves the struggle to separate from the maternal body. Kristeva describes these "earliest attempts to release the hold of the maternal entity even before ex-isting outside of her" as "a violent, clumsy breaking away, with a constant risk of falling back under the sway of a power as securing as it is stifling."[17] To the pre-egological child, the mother, who is not yet a separate entity or an object of consciousness, appears only as "abject"; that is to say, as "a magnet of desire and hatred, fascination and disgust" (TL 374/464). Thus, the archaic process of separation is an ambiguous movement, because as the infant attempts to free himself from the maternal hold he remains fundamentally dependent upon, what Kristeva calls, the "maternal container" for its very existence.[18]

We will also show that the success of this separation from the maternal is dependent on another movement—that of *transference* to the place of the "third." To make sense of this movement, it is necessary to first make a few prefatory remarks about the word "transference" and Kristeva's usage of it. This term, as is well-known, is borrowed from psychoanalysis and has a technical meaning relating to the therapeutic process. In analysis, a patient will displace his affects for a previous, in fact primordial, love object onto the person of the analyst. The analyst, who is essentially a stranger, becomes a substitute for an archaic, idealized Other. In this therapeutic reenactment of the love relation, the patient is able to repeat, work through, and hence renegotiate an original love traumatism, ideally restructuring his very subjectivity. Although Freud recognized the power of transference love within the analytic or therapeutic setting, Kristeva believes that he never fully thought through its potential for an understanding of subjectivity itself.[19] Kristeva argues that such therapeutic transference is only possible because the *first experience* (if we can rightly call it an "experience," since there is not yet an "I" to take account of it, or "first," since the "I" only comes to know anything of *this* transference through later ones) of love—of being loved and of loving oneself—is a movement of transference.

The "first" instance of transference, which will be repeated in every amatory relationship, occurs when the infant, who is in the throes of separating from the maternal, identifies with and incorporates the speech of the third. It seems, then, that Kristeva's emerging subject will have more in common with Ovid's Echo than the scopophilic Narcissus, which will significantly distinguish her account of subject formation from Lacan's. And it is through this process of oral assimilation (where words and sounds reverberate) in which the child is carried over to the site of the third and takes himself for this ideal Other, that a kind of transference or substitution is effected. We will find that, thanks to transference, a space or an emptiness is opened up within the psyche, allowing the imagination to take shape. This space of imagination, which is composed of a range of perceptions and representations (and not simply visual images), gives rise to necessary fictions that will form the core of an individual's identity.

In becoming *like* the loving Other, who appears to the child as One, the child begins to love himself and take up a *"position of subjectivity,"* which is defined by Kristeva as "a being for and by the Other" (NMS 122/183). Therefore, we learn that the movement toward individuation, which can only take place through loving identification and transference, entails that the "I" lose itself in the Other and find itself (transformed) in and through this Other.

In Chapter 4, "Transference, or Amorous Dynamics," we find the subject, which is for Kristeva forever *en procès*, repeatedly caught up in the movement of transference; that is to say, undergoing metamorphoses. In this chapter, we consider the repetition of the transferential or "metaphorical" movement in two similar, yet distinct, scenes: first, that of the lover's discourse and, second, that of analytic discourse. In each case, be it "love as transference" or "transference (as) love," narcissistic identification and idealization must be renegotiated, as narcissism is, according to Kristeva, the *prime mover* for love. Thus love's discourse, which is always already narcissistic, opens up the flow of heterogeneity (that is, a greater fluidity between the realms of the semiotic and symbolic) within language and consequently engenders transformation and renewal within the self. Indeed, as this chapter will demonstrate, Kristeva makes the case that the transferential relationship, which inextricably intertwines self-love and love of the other, "is a true process of self-organization (*un véritable processus d'auto-organisation*)" and, as such, a source of renewal and creativity (TL 14/24).

CHAPTER 3

Reconceiving Freud's Narcissus

The hypothesis of Narcissus is crucial to this Freudian course . . . Freud seems to suggest that it is not Eros but narcissistic primacy that sparks and perhaps dominates psychic life.

—*Tales of Love*

THE OMNIPRESENCE OF NARCISSISM

In order to make sense of the complex relationship between Eros and Narcissus, between love of the other and love of self, we must retrace the steps in Kristeva's return to Freud in which she unfolds and reworks his complex notion of narcissism. Kristeva's reading reveals that, in his writings, Freud radically reconfigures the Narcissus of the tradition and "surreptitiously rehabilitate[s] narcissism" (TL 123/155). In doing so, Freud finds the face of Narcissus not only on "perverts" and "inverts" but also on "every living creature" (SE 14:74). This latter form of narcissism, which Freud dubs "primary and normal narcissism," is now part of the natural course of each individual's psychosexual development (SE 14:74). Kristeva also observes that for Freud this "omnipresence of narcissism" extends beyond the confines of the ego and "permeates the other realms to the point that one finds it again in the object (where it is reflected)" (TL 22/32). Since Freud in many of his texts, most notably in "On Narcissism," "binds the state of loving to narcissism," erotic love expresses itself as another incarnation of childhood or primary narcissism, in which a subject's narcissism is reborn in the figure of the love object (TL 21/31).

Summarizing Freud's depiction of narcissism in the erotic life of the sexes in Part II of his 1914 essay, Kristeva writes that

> the choice of the love object, be it *"narcissistic"* or *"anaclitic,"* proves satisfying in any case if and only if that object relates to the subject's narcissism in one of two ways: (1) loving according to the "narcissistic-type" (where Narcissus is the subject—for Freud, that would be woman), or (2) loving according to the "anaclitic-type" (where Narcissus is the other).[1] (TL 21/31–32)

Thus, in Freud's account, an adult loves in one of two ways, either narcissistically or anaclitically, that is to say, an individual either libidinally invests in himself or in an other as his sexual object. Theoretically speaking, Freud contends that every individual, because he originally had two objects of desire ("himself and the woman who nurse[d] him"), may give preference to — either type of object choice (SE 14:88). However, as Kristeva notes in the above passage, woman (or, in Freud's own words, "the type of female most frequently met with, which is probably the truest one") is unable to transfer her primary narcissism onto an external object and thus cannot rediscover it reflected in the love object.[2] Therefore, when Freud's Narcissus appears as a "subject," he most frequently appears as a woman (or occasionally as a homosexual, i.e., a feminized man). When Narcissus emerges as an object of desire or, in Kristeva's words, as an other, he also wears the visage of a woman; because, on Freud's account, the majority of men transform their primary narcissism into "[c]omplete object-love of the attachment type," which is marked by the transfer of infantile narcissism and its accompanying fantasies of perfection onto the beloved. Man's libidinal investments are thus redirected away from his own ego toward an external object, at the expense of impoverishing his own ego (SE 14:88). Whether as subject or object, ego or other, Narcissus, after nearly two thousand years as a pubescent male, undergoes a sex change. This, however, is another story—one that Kristeva only alludes to in her minor history of narcissism.[3] Therefore, we will put aside this curious shift for another time.[4]

Although the two sexes would, according to Freud, typically travel along different paths of desire, a narcissistic destiny would be presupposed in all loves, object choices, and libidinal investments. Yet, despite the ubiquity of the notion of narcissism in Freud's writings, Kristeva correctly notes that Freud, adopting a tone so common in the history of Western metaphysics, attempts to retreat from this narcissistic destiny that he has so convincingly sketched out "in favor of a 'true' object choice," that is to say, in favor of attachment love which is, as we just saw, the form of love seen most commonly in men (TL 21/32).[5] Nevertheless, the "sexual overvaluation" of the object that accompanies and distinguishes "the peculiar state of being in love" does not indicate an absence of narcissism but rather reveals its rebirth in the guise of the other. Even further, Kristeva points out, that "on closer examination even [Freud's] Ego Ideal, which insures the transference of our claims and desires toward a true object laden with all the pomp of good and beauty as defined by parental and social codes, is a revival of narcissism, its abeyance, its conciliation, its consolation" (TL 21–22/32). Therefore, Kristeva concludes that in Freud's writings, despite his own hesitations, equivocations, and justifications, it is Narcissus rather than Eros who ignites and animates psychic life.

BEYOND AUTOEROTICISM: THE NARCISSISTIC SUPPLEMENT

The ubiquity of "narcissism" in the works of Freud indicates to Kristeva that narcissism is not originary but rather supplementary. In her reading, Kristeva highlights the fact that Freud describes "primary narcissism" as a "new psychical action" that is added onto or supplements an originary autoeroticism. As early as the *Three Essays on the Theory of Psychoanalysis*, Freud contends that the autoerotic instincts, in which the libidinal pleasure that is at first bound up with the activities (nursing, defecating, urinating) that make an infant's survival possible, are turned toward the child's own body and are repeated independently of any vital function (e.g., sensual sucking, anal scratching, masturbation).[6] However, in "On Narcissism," Freud seems to suggest that the autoerotic instincts do not chronologically follow, in a kind of developmental progression, but rather appear to be coextensive with them, when he writes "[t]he autoerotic instincts, however, are there from the start" (SE 14:77). Although Freud maintains that the child is always already autoerotic—that is to say, the infant takes pleasure in his own body—he does not describe such libidinal satisfaction as narcissistic. Nor does Freud depict the libidinal attachment an infant has to his mother as narcissistic.

Kristeva concurs with Freud that primary narcissism can neither be found in the child's merging with his mother nor in the child's preoccupation with autoerotic pleasures. Rather, Freud insists "there must be something to add to autoeroticism—a new psychical action [*eine neue psychische Aktion*]—in order to bring about narcissism" (SE 14:77). Likewise, Kristeva maintains that narcissism is hardly originary in the life of a speaking being. Instead, she suggests that it emerges as "a third realm supplementing the autoeroticism of the mother-child dyad" (TL 22/33). Thus, the apparent fullness of the mother-child dyad (which has so often been viewed as the seat of all narcissism) requires a supplement—a third—for there to be any narcissism and, consequently, any identity. Narcissism, unlike autoeroticism, which lacks an object or an other (and hence an image), is neither a symbiotic state nor a dyadic structure.

Narcissism, according to Kristeva, necessarily involves a third term or pole, an outside of or a beyond the two, which prevents a lethal fusion between mother and child and permits individuation. Narcissus thus will emerge out of a pre-Oedipal ternary structure, which is made up of (1) the child or, as Kristeva often refers to him, the "narcissistic subject," (2) his mother, and (3) a "third," which appears as an archaic figure of a loving father.[7] In her account, Narcissus can only be born within the tenuous space opened up between these two poles, that is, between the maternal body and the "third party." Yet, this space is neither preestablished nor permanent; the space itself must be given birth to as Narcissus separates from his mother and begins his fledgling identification with a third party.

MAKING SPACE FOR NARCISSUS: BETWEEN ABJECTION AND IDEALIZATION
Abjection and the Maternal

Abjection [. . .] is a precondition of narcissism. It is coexistent with it and causes it to be permanently brittle.

—*Powers of Horror*

Let us turn briefly to Kristeva's *Powers of Horror: An Essay on Abjection*, in which she traces the violent and visceral movements of Narcissus in his struggle for separation from the maternal. In pulling away from his mother, Narcissus attempts to open up a space that will be essential for his singularity and identity. *Powers of Horror*, as Sara Beardsworth rightly notes, "presents [us with] the most confusing aspect of the narcissistic structure [. . .] the moment of subjectivity closest to irrationality" (SB 82). In order to address the most perplexing moment of the narcissistic structure, we must first recall the "immemorial violence with which a body becomes separated from another body in order to be" (PH 10/17). This scene of primordial separation involves an "I" who is "not yet," but is nonetheless touched, affected, and shaped by what does not appear to it as an object or an entity.

Before there is "an other with whom I identify and incorporate," an other whom I become *like*, there is, Kristeva writes, an "Other who precedes and possesses me, and through such possession causes me to be" (PH 10/18). This possession, which comes before the advent of my ego or my identity entails "an immersion

in that which is not 'one's own'" (NMS 118/178). The hold that
the Other has on me, who is not yet properly an "I," structures
my very existence: "That order, that glance, that voice, that
gesture [. . .] enact[s] the law for my frightened body" (PH
10/17). This "not-yet I" is held and hence conditioned by a maternal order and its "structures of meaning" (PH 10/17). Kristeva
proposes that the "possession previous to my advent," where each
touch and word functions as my law, is an already "being-there
of the symbolic" (PH 10/18). If this order, which weaves affect
and the symbolic together, inhabits my body, then, for Kristeva,
significance must be "inherent in the human body" (PH 10/18).

Yet, this Other, who comes before me, who conditions the parameters of my existence, and who causes me to be, also threatens to devour me or forever hold me in its death grip—preventing
the process of my individuation and thwarting my chance
to live.

The "overwhelming presence of the mother," her "close proximity with the child," has the potential to stifle the opening up
of space for imaginary and symbolic elaboration to fully take
place (PK 333). Therefore, Kristeva insists that "abjection" of
the maternal, in all its ambiguity, is a necessary precondition for
any narcissism; that is, in order for the "I" to be *like* an other, to
identify with a loving third party, it is essential that it also
"separate, reject, ab-ject" the maternal (PH 13/21). The maternal, therefore, appears to the child as an "ambiguous object" or,
more precisely, as a pre-object that is both a "magnet of fascination and repulsion," causing the child to alternate between
fusion and rejection (NMS 118/178). It is only through this revolt "against" the maternal that a space in which signs and objects can arise will be demarcated. However, this most elementary
form of separation can only succeed with the "assistance of the
so-called pre-Oedipal mother" (TL 40/55).

However, Kristeva credits the emergence of Narcissus's identity, as well as his capacity for love, to his identification with the
archaic appearance of a third party and not to the protection
provided by the enveloping skin of the maternal body. In a con-

troversial claim, Kristeva asserts that "[i]f love stems from narcissistic identification, it has nothing to do with the protective wrapping over skin and sphincters that maternal care provides for the baby" (TL 34/48). Yet, Kristeva also insists that the infant's success or failure to separate from the maternal—an impossible separation if there ever was one—is largely dependent on the mother's own desire for another. Parting with conventional notions of maternal love, Kristeva splits the figure of the mother in two, distinguishing what she will call "the caring and clinging mother" from "the loving mother" (TL 34/48). In the case of the former, all of the mother's desire is directed toward and invested in her child, whom she encloses in a kind of "adhesive maternal wrapping" (TL 35/49). Kristeva warns that "if that protection continues, if the mother 'clings' to her offspring [. . .] the chances are that neither love nor psychic life will ever hatch from such an egg" (TL 34/48). It is important to note that this evocation of the overdetermined image of the egg symbolizes, for Kristeva, neither a benign form of maternal love, which envelops and thus protects her offspring, nor a malignant and contemptible form of infantile narcissism. Rather, she employs the figure of the unhatched egg to depict the dangers that autoeroticism presents to mother and child alike, what she describes as a lethal "osmosis as well as the merciless war where self-destruction alternates with the destruction of the other" (SNS 54/86).[8] Indeed, without the splitting of the shell, there is no chance for life and love—for a life of love—to ever hatch from this egg.[9]

Maternal Desire and the Third

[T]he advent of the *Vater der persönlichen Vorzeit* takes place thanks to the assistance of the so-called pre-Oedipal mother. . . .

—*Tales of Love*

It is Kristeva's contention that the psychic life of the child has a chance to survive if the mother desires another, someone other than her child. It is precisely this desire for and love of an other—beyond the mother-child dyad—that will introduce a

supplement to this "couple." By desiring an outside of the autoerotic mother-child pair (which is, accurately speaking, not truly
a pair until the third enters) and by turning toward a third party,
Kristeva's "loving mother" calls the pre-Oedipal triad into existence. And, Kristeva argues, this is "for a very good reason, since
without that disposition of the psyche, the child and the mother
do not yet constitute 'two'" (TL 40/56). As we will see, it will be
the third party that will serve as "the guarantee of a love relationship between the mother and the child" (PK 334).

The mother's desire for another, writes Kristeva, "indicate[s]
to her child that her desire is not limited to responding to her
offspring's request (or simply turning it down)" (TL 40/55). The
third toward which the mother's desire is directed serves as "an
indication [to the child] that the mother is not complete but
that she wants . . . Who? What? The question has no answer
other than the one that uncovers narcissistic emptiness; 'At
any rate, not I'" (TL 41/56). Therefore, this maternal "diversion"
toward a third party will assist the infant in the process of individuation by fracturing its fantasy of autoeroticism, thus opening up a space in which Narcissus can be loved. It is, therefore,
"with respect to the Other" and "through a discourse aimed at
that Third Party that the child will be set up as 'loved' for the
mother," because the maternal discourse that addresses itself to
a third party forms a "verbal backdrop" for Narcissus to emerge
on the scene (TL 34/48). Paradoxically, then, it is only in turning away from her child and toward an other that the mother
can make her love for her child manifest and can create the
conditions for him to begin to love himself.

"The Zero Degree of the Third"

And this zero degree is not a word used by Freud; I use the word, Freud
speaks about the father of pre-individual history, which is not grasped as a
real person by the infant but like a sort of symbolic instance; something that
is here that cannot be here—the possibility of absence, the possibility of love,
the possibility of interdiction but also of a gift.

—"Julia Kristeva in Conversation with Rosalind Coward"

In order to separate from the maternal, the "narcissistic subject" will need to gravitate toward the "third," which is neither an object of desire nor an object of cognition, but rather a loving pole that draws the child toward itself. Kristeva casts this third pole or party as an archaic appearance of the "paternal function" that precedes the Name, the Law, and the Symbolic, borrowing from Freud this strange figure of "the father of individual prehistory" that will play such a pivotal role in the birth of the subject and, consequently, in the formation of his "ego ideal." As Freud explains in Part III of *The Ego and the Id*, behind the ego ideal "there lies hidden an individual's *first and most important identification*, his identification with the father in his own personal prehistory."[10] At first glance, it appears that Freud is suggesting that Narcissus's first identification is not with his mother but exclusively with his father. By introducing Freud's figure of the archaic father, Kristeva, we are convinced, is not attempting to designate this figure of primary identification as an empirical father or even as an exclusively male figure. In *Tales of Love*, she openly scoffs at such an archeology of origins: "The problem is not to find an answer to the enigma: who might be the object of primary identification, daddy or mummy? Such an attempt would open an impossible quest for the absolute origin of the capacity for love as a psychic and symbolic capacity" (TL 28/41).

In an interview, Elaine Hoffmann Baruch presses Kristeva with regard to the identity of the third party: Could we then "say that the function of the father has nothing to do with the sex, and that someone female could play the role of separator?" (PK 375). To this line of questioning, Kristeva replies that there is no absolute necessity in labeling these positions "mother" or "father" and adds that one could legitimately refer to these positions as X and Y. Kristeva credits the feminist movement with the opening up of, what she calls, a "baroque space," in which the distinctions between X and Y are no longer rigorously drawn due to a greater contamination between them, rendering these terms ambiguous. Although ideological and historical changes affect the content of these positions, what remains essential for "psychic space to accede to language is the existence of this distance," which can only open up on the basis of three terms (PK 335).

Kristeva turns our attention to a crucial footnote in *The Ego and the Id* that Freud adds to clarify, or perhaps to complicate, the status of this "father of individual prehistory." There, he elaborates: "[I]t would be safer to say [that the first identification is] 'with the parents'; for before a child has arrived at definite knowledge between the sexes [. . .] it does not distinguish in value between its father and mother" (SE 19:31). This "archaic father" is, as Kristeva emphasizes, truly an ambiguous figure, as "he" is a combination of the characteristics of both parents and is "[e]ndowed with the sexual attributes of [each]" (TL 33/47). In *Reading Kristeva: Unraveling the Double-Bind*, Kelly Oliver interprets Kristeva's deployment of Freud's "father of individual prehistory" not as a strengthening of the paternal function to the detriment of the maternal but rather as an undermining or deconstructing of "the maternal/paternal dualism."[11] Oliver's claim can be confirmed by multiple passages in Kristeva's writing in which she refers to this first and most important figure of identification as a "father-mother conglomerate" (TL 40/56) or, reworking Freud's terminology, "a Father-Mother in personal prehistory [*un Père-Mère de la préhistoire individuelle*]" and when she insists that the narcissistic subject "internalizes both parents and both genders" (NMS 122/182–83). What then lies at the core of the narcissistic structure and at the origin of infant's ability to gain access to both the imaginary and symbolic realms is "this two-sided and double-gendered figure of kinship [*cette figure biface et bisexe de la parenté*]" (NMS 122/183).

Further, this ideal Other, which is designated by Kristeva with a series of substitutable terms—the third or the third party [*le Tiers*], primary thirdness [*tiercité primaire*], the third pole [*le pole tiers*], the father of individual prehistory [*le père de la préhistoire individuelle*], the Imaginary Father [*le Père Imaginaire*], and the father-mother conglomerate [*le conglomérat père-mère*]—

not only is without any fixed features and, hence, cannot be determined as either male or female but also cannot be reduced to any empirical entity. Adding another, even more minimal, name to the list of names for this primary pole of identification, Kristeva declares that the "zero degree of the third"—her expression and not Freud's—"is not grasped as a real person by the infant" but rather as "something that is here that cannot be here—the possibility of absence, the possibility of love, the possibility of interdiction but also of a gift" (PK 333). The third, thus, emerges not as an empirical being but as "some sort of archaic occurrence of the symbolic" (PK 334), that is, "[a]s the zero-degree of symbol formation" (NMS 122/183).

TRANSFERENCE AND TRANSFORMATION
Identifying Kristeva's Narcissus as Echo

To refer to our mythology—I mean psychoanalysis—
I would like to know (if this can be known) what happens
when one goes back from Narcissus to Echo.
   —Philippe Lacoue-Labarthe,Typography: Mimesis, Philosophy, Politics

Kristeva's theory of narcissism details how primary identification with the third ultimately gives rise to the narcissistic ego. The origin of this archaic identification is, however, no clearer than is the "object" of this identification. However, agreeing with Freud, she declares that primary identification with the third is "immediate," "direct," and "previous to any concentration on any object whatsoever" (TL 26/38). Further, Kristeva argues, "if there is an *immediacy* of the child's identification with" the third, it is only on the condition that the child does not have to elaborate a relation to the loving third party. Instead, she suggests that the narcissistic child "receives it [the relation to the third], mimics it, or even sustains it through the mother who offers it to him (or refuses it) as a gift" (TL 40/55). Kristeva, thus, likens this gift of identification to the notion of *agape*, which entails an identification with a profuse love that comes

from outside, from above—"as a god send [*tombe du ciel*]"—
that one can never earn or merit (TL 40/56).[12]

Kristeva's fledgling Narcissus, then, comes into being insofar
as he belongs to and identifies with this loving Other. More
precisely, in primary identification, the narcissistic subject, a
"not-yet-identity," "is transferred or rather displaced to the site of
an Other" (TL 41/56), "to the very place from which he is seen
and heard" (TL 36/51). Although primary identification will
serve "as the lining of the visual" and will set up the conditions
for speculation, it must take a detour through speech, or should
we say, through a certain echolalia. Kristeva points out that
"*empirically*, the first affections, the first imitations, and the first
vocalizations [. . .] are directed toward the mother" (TL 27/39).
Yet, she maintains that primary identification is with "the
third." This position, however, "is tenable only if one conceives
of *identification* as being always already within the symbolic
orbit, under the sway of language" (TL 27/39). In other words,
the narcissistic subject comes to be insofar as he identifies "with
an ideal Other who is the speaking other, the other insofar as
he speaks" (TL 35/50). This identification as transference to the
place of the speaking Other will endow narcissism with its "in-
trasymbolic status," by opening up the possibility for distinction, differentiation, and hence signification (TL 22/33).

Kristeva remarks that prior to discovering his image in a sil-
very pool, Ovid's "Narcissus encounters a prefiguration of his
doubling [. . .] in the person of the nymph Echo" (TL 103/132).
Let us recall a passage from the *Metamorphoses* in which Ovid
describes Echo's unique condition: "One day, as he was driving
frightened deer into his nets, Narcissus met a nymph: resound-
ing Echo, one whose speech was so strange; for when she heard
the words of others, she could not keep silent, yet she could not
be the first to speak. Though she still had a body—she was not
just a voice as she still uses it: of the many words her ears have
caught, she just repeats the final part of what she has heard."[13]
A few lines further, Ovid reiterates these words: "But she
cannot begin to speak: her nature has forbidden this; and so

she waits for what her state permits: to catch the sounds that she can then give back with her *own* voice" (Ovid 92, my emphasis).

The "narcissistic subject," like or as Echo, catches the words, or simply the sounds, of the Other and delights in repeating, reproducing, and sending back the music that her ears have caught. In this archaic or primary identification, one finds a dominance of the oral—of the mouth, lips, and tongue. Indeed, the very first form of identification, "degree zero of identity" (SNS 53/85), which remains the paradigm for all subsequent identifications (hysterical, projective, etc.), involves the full pleasures of the oral phase, that is to say, "the joys of chewing, swallowing, [and] nourishing oneself [. . .] with words" (TL 26/37). Like "the *eye*," Kristeva writes, "the *mouth* is the main organ of amorous longing" (TL 104/133). With her mouth, Echo "oralizes" the third by "endow[ing] it [. . .] with the jubilatory latencies of an archaic, maternal tongue. Echolalic, vocalizing, lilting, gestural, muscular, rhythmical" (TL 126/159). In receiving and repeating the other's words, in chewing on and swallowing these sounds, the infant becomes bound to the third in love. In *L'amour de soi et ses avatars*, Kristeva adds that the delight that a child displays in verbal repetition reveals that the child loves herself through learning her mother tongue.[14]

Through this oral assimilation, the other is taken in, incorporated, but not as a whole or as an object, but as rhythmic words, as sounds and signs.[15] The speech of the Other, also, should not be thought of as an object but as a *model* or *pattern* with which the infant identifies repeatedly, endlessly. "When the object that I incorporate is the speech of the other—precisely a nonobject, a pattern, a model—I bind myself to him in a primary fusion, communion, unification. An identification" (TL 26/37).[16] Kristeva insists that this primordial echoing ought not be conceived of as imitation, because imitation or mimesis would require a capacity for comparison which would itself rely on the imagination, and it is precisely the foundations of the imagination that are being laid. Rather, she suggests that we understand the child's echoing as "archaic *reduplication*," as "the internal, recursive, redundant logic of discourse, [. . . as] 'afterspeech' (*dire-après*), which is the identification that sets up love, the sign, and repetition at the heart of the psyche" (TL 25/36).

As Echo nourishes herself on the words of the Other, her desire to devour the Other must "be deferred and displaced to a level one may well call 'psychic'" (TL 26/37). No matter how primitive or archaic is the repression at work here, Kristeva insists that the "narcissistic subject's" libido undergoes some restraint, some displacement, some mediation, for identification and hence for love to be possible. And, this displacement of desire reveals "the very splitting that establishes the psyche and, let us call this splitting 'primal repression,' bends the drive toward the symbolic of an other" (TL 31/45).

"Mystical Metamorphosis"

This [identification] entails a *metaphorical* experience similar to Baudelaire's "mystical metamorphosis," as opposed to a mere comparison. This is precisely the sine qua non condition for the advent of the subject.
    —*New Maladies of the Soul*

In identifying with the third—by internalizing and returning the sounds and signs of the Other—Echo becomes *like* the Other. Poetically, Kristeva portrays the power of these rhythmic repetitions, the "after-speech" characteristic of the narcissistic child, when she writes: "a sound on the fringe of my being, which transfers me to the place of the Other, astray, beyond meaning, out of sight" (TL 37/51).[17] She is suggesting that identification is above all a "movement that causes the advent of the subject insofar as he unites himself with the other and makes himself identical to the other" (NMS 178/264). When Kristeva claims in *New Maladies of the Soul* that primary identification is "a *metaphorical* experience similar to Baudelaire's 'mystical metamorphosis,'" she is employing the term "metaphor" in its Greek sense—as *metapherein* (NMS 178–79/265). The Greek verb *"metapherō"* not only indicates a movement in which one thing is transported or carried over to the place of another, but it also implies an alteration or transformation.[18] Thus the metaphorical experience of being transferred to the site of the Other can also be said to be a metamorphosis for the fledgling subject.

Likewise, Kristeva depicts the third—the pole or "magnet of identification constitutive of identity and [the] condition for that unification"—as "a *metaphorical* object" (TL 29/42). However, one should hear the stress on *metaphorical* rather than on *object*, as the third is neither an object of desire nor an object of cognition for the child. For the third can never be an object as such.[19] Rather, the "metaphorical" function of this ideal instance in the subject's prehistory, because it incites a transference that will be a true transformation, will "insure the advent of a subject for an object" (TL 29/42). Therefore, identification and transference, or, more accurately, identification *as* transference, is the taking up of *"the position of subjectivity,"* which is defined by Kristeva as "a being for and by the Other [*un être pour, par l'Autre*]" (NMS 122/182).

Let us pause for a moment to examine more closely what is involved in this "mystical metamorphosis" in which one exists for, even *as*, the Other. Primary identification, via verbal repetition and oral assimilation, enacts a new merging—one that will allow the child to begin to separate from his fusion with the maternal. The "not-yet-I," caught up in what Kristeva describes as "the hysterical universe of loving identification," takes himself, that is to say *mistakes* himself, for the third (TL 34/48). In this intensely affective experience that Kristeva likens to Freud's notion of *"Einfühlung,* the *empathy* that is characteristic of certain amatory, hysterical, or mystical states," the "I" not only finds itself transported to the site of the Other but also becomes *one* with this Other (NMS 178/264). As "an *other* whose [apparent] immutability provides me with a guide and a representation," I am transformed into "a subject capable of preverbal and verbal representations" (NMS 173/257). Indeed, what is at stake in transference is a metamorphosis in which the

preverbal child—the *infans*—becomes capable of heterogeneous representations.

Kristeva argues that the "archaic vortex of idealization" and
identification "gives rise to a powerful, already psychic transference of the previous semiotic body in the process of becoming a narcissistic Ego" (TL 33/47–48). In other words, as the
narcissistic subject identifies with an ideal other and thus undergoes a transference between himself and the third, a transport between the somatic and psychic takes place. As the logic
of identification is "always *unstable* and in *motion*," there is
permeability and fluidity between, what Kristeva designates,
the realms of the semiotic and the symbolic (NMS 179/266).
Thus, she points out that although affects and drives dominate
in narcissistic identification (as they do in all forms of identification), verbal and drive representatives mingle together and are
given expression. Therefore, Kristeva stresses the heterogeneity
that characterizes primary identification when, employing the
language of Lacan, she contends that transference traverses
"the entire range of the symbolic, imaginary, and then real"
(NMS 178/264). And, one finds in primary or narcissistic identification neither a "pre-imaginary" nor a "pre-symbolic" self,
but rather, as we have been attempting to demonstrate, a being
in which a "symbolic sensuality [*une sensualité immédiatement
symbolique*] attempts to take shape" (TL 125/158).

The Object of Narcissism: Psychic Space

It is a new object, which is not mommy or daddy, the breast or any other external erotic object, or the body itself, but an artificial, internal object that
Narcissus is capable of producing: his own representations, speech, sounds,
colors, and so forth.

—*The Sense and Non-Sense of Revolt*

As we have witnessed, for the "I" to become itself, to become
singular, the "I" must first become an other. The transference to
the place of the third, which enacts a separation from the maternal container, allows "emptiness" to open up within the child.

This emptiness is nothing more than a space hollowed out by "the first separation between what is not yet an *Ego* and what is not yet an *object*" (TL 24/35). Kristeva concludes that it is "in the uncertainty of this disengagement [that] an imaginary space is sketched out," which will begin to be filled with images and identifications that will come to constitute the child's narcissistic Ego. Yet, we must pause to ask: How does Kristeva's Narcissus—who doubles as Echo—develop a self-image, an Ego Ideal, through speech alone? How does it happen that "echolalia" passes over into imagination? How does sound shift into sight?

Kristeva demonstrates in *Tales of Love* that the space opened up by Echo's endless word play is indeed imaginary, imaginary not in the sense of make-believe (although it is that as well), but rather in the sense of the production of images. Although Kristeva agrees with Freud and Lacan that narcissism entails a fascination with and investment in one's own image, she refuses to characterize a subject's self-image and the imaginary realm as wholly constituted by the specular.[20] By attending to the formation of the imaginary, which requires a detailed account of the archaic stages of development (i.e., the pre-Oedipal stages), Kristeva reworks the notion of the imaginary in a way that is at once more comprehensive and more precise. As opposed to many of her psychoanalytic predecessors, she emphasizes that "the grasping of the image by the child" can only be thought as "a result of the whole process" of early development (PK 333).

More specifically, Kristeva argues that the process of identification with the ideal Other is paramount in creating the conditions for the child's imagination to spring forth. As previously noted, narcissistic identification, like every form of identification, passes primarily through the mouth and ear. If this is the case, then the imaginary cannot be comprised solely of the visual (as it is commonly thought), but also must include the oral and auditory. Kristeva writes: "as for the image making up this 'imagination,' it should not be conceived as simply visual but as [. . .] corresponding to the entire gamut of perceptions, especially *sonorous* ones" (TL 40/56). It is instructive to return for a moment to Ovid's "Echo and Narcissus," where we find a linguistic parallel drawn between two forms of reflection—one auditory and one visual.[21] In the *Metamorphoses*, Ovid not only designates the reflection that Narcissus sees in the water with the word *imago* but also uses the locution *imago vocis* to depict the auditory reflection or echo that returns to Narcissus. Therefore, each form of reflection is an *imago* and belongs to the order of the imaginary. Despite the linguistic and structural similarity between these two forms of the image in Ovid's text, Kristeva clearly gives primacy to sound and speech over sight in the birth of the narcissistic subject, for she believes that these infinite echoes of the other's words "in the final analysis, shape the visible, hence fantasy" (TL 37/51).

In primary identification, it is the play of sonorous images, "in the dizziness of rebounds," that ultimately "reveals itself as a screen over emptiness" (TL 23/34). Drawing on the work of the French psychoanalyst André Green, Kristeva envisions a psychic emptiness that emerges out of narcissistic identification. We thus find emptiness and narcissism involved in a strange solidarity, where "the one uphold[s] the other, constitut[ing] the zero degree of imagination" (TL 24/35). On the one hand, narcissism "protects emptiness, causes it to exist, and thus, as the lining of that emptiness, insures an elementary separation" (TL 24/35). On the other hand, the narcissistic subject is threatened by and attempts to exorcise the very same emptiness that permits him to hear and see himself as other, as ideal. Through the "whole contrivance of imagery, representations, identifications, and projections," Narcissus transforms this frightening, yet indispensable, void into a source for self-identity (TL 42/57). Therefore, "[n]arcissism would be that correlation (with the imaginary father and the ab-jected mother) enacted around a central emptiness of that transference. [And] emptiness [. . .] is apparently the primer of the symbolic function" (TL 42/57). Thus, without this paradoxical play "between emptiness and narcissism" that is supported by the third, Kristeva claims that fusion with the maternal "would sweep away any possibility of distinction, trace, and symbolization," and with it any possibility of singularity, identity, and love (TL 24/35).

Kristeva concludes that the narcissistic subject has only one true object: "The object of Narcissus is psychic space; it is representation itself, fantasy" (TL 116/147). In other words, "psychic space" is the space of imagination, where seeming is not opposed to being, but rather where seeming *is* being. This "narcissistic seeming," which deploys all types of images—sonorous, tactile, visual—is the site where Narcissus and his Ego Ideal are born. Through loving identification, *having* or possessing the words of the other has shifted over to *being* or becoming *like* the Other—singular, one, a "subject of enunciation" (TL 26/38). Unlike Ovid, and other inheritors of Plato, Kristeva locates image, illusion, and "mere seeming" at the core of the truth of self-identity. And, once again, she credits Freud for being the first to "set up self-deception at the basis of one's relationship to reality" and for showing that these indispensable illusions are and ought to be "rehabilitated, neutralized, normalized, at the bosom of my loving reality" (TL 21/31), allowing "the official fiction that constitutes [. . .] subjective identity" to commence (NMS 184/272).

CHAPTER 4

Transference, or Amorous Dynamics

LOVE AS TRANSFERENCE

Love is a necessary seeming, which is to be restored, aroused, promoted endlessly.

— *Tales of Love*

After so persuasively demonstrating that self-love is not reducible to a moral value or a medical symptom but rather that it is a complex organization that enables the emerging subject to take shape and to truly live, it would only make sense that Kristeva would not portray Eros as an anti-Narcissus and depict love of the other as wholly distinct or severed from love of the self. Kristeva, like a certain Freud, resists the overly simplistic and naïve opposition that has so often been set up between Eros and Narcissus and, instead, claims that the lover is another incarnation of the narcissist, "a narcissist with an *object*" to be exact (TL 33/47). In spite of the differences between love and narcissism, Kristeva stresses the continuity between the two forms of love.[1] Perhaps, it is more precise to say that love, which "is initially [and, perhaps, essentially] narcissistic," repeats the movement of loving identification and transference that is central to narcissism (TL 124/157). And, in this sense, Narcissus is the "prime mover (*moteur*) [. . .] for love" (TL 124/156).[2]

As was noted in the introduction to Part II, Kristeva insists that all love discourses have not denied but "dealt with narcissism" and, thus, integrated self-love into their erotic ideals (TL 7/16). This is because all "[a]matory experience rests on *narcissism* and on its aura of emptiness, seeming and impossibility, which underlies any *idealization*" (TL 267/331). In fact, Kristeva asserts that love flourishes between, what she calls, "the two borders of *narcissism* and *idealization*" (TL 6/16). In other words, the narcissistic structure that generates self-love via idealizing the third can be logically, although not experientially, divided into these two essential elements that universally appear in every love, regardless of its particular configuration or orchestration (friendship, erotic, homosexual, heterosexual, etc.). Although this division between narcissism and idealization appears reminiscent of, if not identical to, Freud's split of libido into ego-libido and object-libido, that is, into narcissistic and anaclitic love, what Kristeva is highlighting is that each and every instance of love is inevitably bound up with both. Thus, in love the "emphasis may be put in [one] situation more on violence, or more on narcissism, or more on idealization, or more on the erotic, and so on. But the two components: narcissism and idealization will last, will endure" (PK 337).

Let us then examine how these two inseparable aspects of the narcissistic structure find themselves reenacted in the experience of love. Like the narcissistic child, the lover finds himself getting carried away. Self-love, as we witnessed in the previous chapter, is engendered in the child insofar as he identifies with and is transferred to the place where the "I" is loved by the Other, by the third. "The first variant of identification," Kristeva writes in *Sense and Non-Sense of Revolt*, "recurs with amorous idealization in the lover's discourse" (SNS 52/84). In amorous identification, the Ego Ideal, its "Highness the Ego," "projects and glorifies itself, or else shatters into pieces and is engulfed, when it admires itself in the mirror of an idealized Other" (TL 7/16). It is therefore this narcissistic capacity to project oneself "through the ideal instance and to identify with it" that Kristeva terms *idealization* (PK 337). Clearly idealization is inseparable from narcissism, as the "I" projects its *own* ideal image (itself an imaginary construction based on the child's first and most influential identification with the father-mother conglomeration in personal prehistory) onto the beloved only to have it returned to him, revealing an "exorbitant aggrandizement of the loving Self as extravagant in its pride as in its humility" (TL 4/13).

Thus, amorous projection is a repetition of transference in which the lover is carried over to the place of the loved one; that is, the idealized Other. In this revival of narcissism, the lover "imagine[s] himself similar, merging with [the beloved], and even indistinguishable from him" (TL 33/47). Hence, Kristeva defines love as "the merging of the identifying ideal with the object of desire" (TL 32/46). Once again, loving identification (in truth, is there any other?) leads the "I" into the rapturous terrain of transference in which the "I" will have been an *other*. All the while the "I" echoes the language of love (for "I" am not the first nor the last to utter the words "I love you"), which is, according to Kristeva, "impossible, inadequate, immediately allusive when one would like it to be straightforward; it is a flight of metaphors" (TL 1/9). Therefore, while under the sway of love and caught up in the lover's discourse, the "I," which is paradoxically both expanded and annihilated *as* other, never speaks *of* his love. For, the temporality of love as transference— and this holds true for the "first" or "primordial" instance of transference—is a sort of "nontime," "both instant and eternity" that simultaneously "fulfills me [and] abolishes me" (TL 6/15) and "of which one speaks of only *after the fact* [*on ne parle qu'*après-coup]" (TL 3/12). Thus, Kristeva concludes, the transferential experience, whether it be experienced as narcissistic or amatory identification, occurs "in a sort of future perfect [*une sorte de futur antèrieur*]" (TL 6/15).

In this maelstrom of words and affect, "the limits of one's own identity vanishes, at the same time that the precision of reference and meaning becomes blurred in love's discourse (of which Barthes has so elegantly written the *Fragments*)" (TL 2/10). Like the narcissistic child's echolalia, the lover's discourse opens up and "manifest[s] the semiotic flow within symbolicity" (TL 16/27). Thus, the heterogeneity that the experience of love, that is to say, transference (for Kristeva uses "love" and "transference" more or less synonymously), elicits in the self a transformation or metamorphosis. "[T]he state of love is such a disconcerting dynamic," yet, as Kristeva writes, it is for the subject "the supreme guarantee of renewal" (TL 16/27). Thus, "the dynamic value of the transferential or love relationship" (TL 123/156) is its capacity to generate a rebirth—making "us good as new, temporarily and eternally" (TL 381/473).

TRANSFERENCE (AS) LOVE

Freud, the post-Romanticist, was the first to turn love into a cure; he did this, not to allow one to grasp a truth, but to provoke a rebirth.

   —*Tales of Love*

When Kristeva writes, in the opening pages of *Tales of Love*, that "[t]heologies and literatures, beyond sin and fiendish characters, invite us to carve out our own territory within love, establish ourselves as *particular [propre]*, outdo ourselves in a sublime Other," she seems to be extolling the virtues of these narratives as models for the formation of the self (TL 7/16). In particular, she has often in her writings approvingly examined the map that Christianity sketched out for subjectivity.[3] So much so, that one may begin to wonder if Kristeva's psychoanalytic interpretation of self-love and love of the other is nothing but a resurrection of the Christian paradigm in the guise of a secular (or Jewish) science. This suspicion seems to be fully confirmed when one reads the following passage from *New Maladies of the Soul*:

> It is nevertheless a fact that John [the Baptist's] reflection offers psychoanalysis an exemplary course of action. By beginning with the sign-gift that subjects "the people" to the power of an Other, John's thought develops a two-tiered theory of love-identification (between Jesus and God, between the believer and Jesus) that serves as a foundation for a complex subjectivity [. . .]. From that point on, the sign acts as a more-than-metaphor: a transport of the father, a hold on the violence of affects, a revival of infinite interpretive activity, and a return to corporeal identity. (NMS 132–33/199)

The similarities between Kristeva's depiction of the Christian paradigm for identity (via the *agape* of the Cross) and her own psychoanalytic model for the optimum evolution of the self (via transference love) are certainly striking. Is Kristeva's philosophy of (self-)love ultimately motivated by religious nostalgia and, by extension, a prescription for a return to the stable and reassuring ideals provided by the Christian narrative? Did she not claim, in the oft-quoted passage, that "today we lack being *particular* [propre], covered as we are with so much abjection, because the guideposts that insured our ascent toward the good have been proven questionable, we have crises of love?" (TL 7/16). The absence of "a code of love" or "stable mirrors for the loves for a period, group, or class" is largely the result of the breakdown of "metanarratives" (to borrow the language of Lyotard) or, at least, to their weakening hold over cultural imagination.

Yet, Kristeva denies that her interest in Christianity is driven by a conservative desire: "When I spoke about love and stressed Christianity, for me that's not nostalgia. It's more a questioning about the discourse that can take the place of this religious discourse that is cracking now. And I don't think political discourse can take its place" (PK 341). In what sounds like a hubristic declaration, Kristeva asserts that the only contemporary discourse that addresses the ego as affective and its quest for (self-)love is the language of psychoanalysis. By extension, she believes that the sole space that is socially consecrated to this search is the private sphere of the analyst's office. Some troubling questions then arise: Is Kristeva calling for the erection of a new Ideal, with well-demarcated borders, that offers safety, security, even salvation, like the religious codes of the days of old? Does psychoanalysis propose, like a new religion, to take over where the previous narratives left off?

At the close of her major work on love, Kristeva poses a series of questions about the status, as well as the stakes, of psychoanalysis. She asks:

> Are we [analysts] to rebuild a psychic space, a certain mastery of the One [*une certaine maîtrise de l'Un*], at the very heart of the psychic founderings of anguished, suicidal, and impotent people? Or on the contrary are we to follow, impel, favor breakaways, driftings? Are we concerned with rebuilding their own proper space, a "home," for contemporary Narcissi: repair the father, soothe the mother, allow them to build a solid introspective inside, master of its losses and wanderings [*maître de ses pertes et de ses errances*], assuming that such a goal is attainable? (TL 379/470)

Kristeva insists that the analyst ought not seek to provide the analysand with the outline of a proper self, "filling it with the psychological meaning of our interpretations" (TL 380/471). Eschewing the position of authority and mastery, Kristeva's analyst will not be the warden or guardian of the self's borders. Nor will psychoanalysis "inaugurate a new amatory code," secular or religious (as if such a distinction were even tenable); rather, psychoanalysis "asserts the end of codes" (TL 382/473).

Although the analyst will not impose a new ideal on her analysands, she is nonetheless "duty bound to help them in building their own proper space," to help them turn their "crisis into a work in progress" (TL 380/471). It is her task to assist her patients to "speak and write themselves in unstable, open, undecidable spaces" rather than to conform to the preestablished contours of some subjective unity (TL 380/471). Kristeva, therefore, advocates that the *seeming* that self-love gives rise to be taken seriously and invested in without guilt, the guilt that arises from a lack of a stable image and "the transcendental Unity that insures its authenticity" (380/472). It is only "[w]hen behaviors and institutions will have integrated the [so-called] failure of representation not as a misfire on the part of the machine or a suffering of the individual, but as an illusion among others" that, Kristeva claims, "a new adjustment of narcissism will be affected (*un nouveau réglage du narcissisme aura eu lieu*)" (TL 380/472).

Rather than attempting to set him straight, the analyst will assist the analysand in reconfiguring and integrating "seemings" and other so-called "errors." If the success, even the "truth," of psychoanalysis "lies in its ability to absorb seemings" (TL 380–81/472), then how does such an analytic cure come about? Kristeva proposes that we turn to the "imagination as the antidote of the crisis," since the imagination (as we witnessed earlier in the chapter) "is a discourse of transference—of love" (TL 381/472). Therefore love, that is, "amorous transference," "produces the dynamic effects of the cure" (TL 125/158). Although differently configured, transference love, like narcissistic and erotic transference, is a dynamic involving three poles: "the *subject* (the analysand), his imaginary or real *object* (the other with whom what is being played out is the whole intersubjective drama of neurosis or, in more severe cases, of the disintegration of the identity leading to psychosis), and the *Third Party*, the stand-in for the potential Ideal, possible Power" (TL 13/23). The part of loving third party is played by the analyst, "who could be," Kristeva adds, a "woman psychotherapist" (PK 375).

Kristeva insists that the love that is essential to therapeutic renewal can never be one-sided, but that it must be double-sided. Although differently positioned, both the analysand (in the position of the narcissistic subject) and the analyst (in the position of the third party) must be caught up in love if there is to be analysis. Kristeva thus issues a warning to the analyst who ignores or dismisses the transferential dynamic (which necessarily includes countertransference): "The analyst is within love from the start, and if he forgets it he dooms himself not to perform an analysis" (TL 13/23). Kristeva recalls that it was Freud who first revealed that "this double-sided desire could be detected in a *discourse* addressed, through transference, toward the analyst-Other," making "the *ear* the most important organ" (MK 9/16). In turning love into a cure, the analyst opens up transference, which (re)occurs through loving identification and hence renews the importance of the interplay between the oral and aural. It is no surprise, then, that the words and sounds that reverberate between analyst and analysand are central to this reorganization or "re-elaboration" of the self.

Therapeutic re-elaboration necessarily entails *repetition*— not only of scenes (reenactments of previous loves and losses) but also of signs (composed of a heterogeneous range of representations, in all their affective richness). This repetition, however, ought not be confused with mere repetition or even traumatic repetition, which "would be something morbid" (PK 343). Rather, Kristeva says that in this re-elaboration "[t]here is a part of repetition and there is a new part which is added and which makes this transference a sort of innovation" (PK 343). Moreover, in transference love "simple repetition [. . .] never occurs because in every transference there is something new that happens" (PK 343). For within the transference dynamic, what were once accidents or errors within "a finalistic linear process that anguished me before" are no longer experienced as failures, but rather they "are overcompensated [and] produce the libidinal self-organization that has an effect of making me more complex and autonomous" (TL 14/24).

We must, once again, underscore that transference and its power to "overcompensate" and give new form and significance to the "errors" of one's life is not equivalent to the imposition of a new Ideal in which I am rendered "whole." Rather, in emphasizing that the "I" is nothing other than a number of "failed identifications as well as my impossible attempts to be an autonomous being" and that, despite all my best efforts, "I am never ideally One under the Law of the Other," the self is able through transference love (whether this take place on the analyst's couch, through aesthetic activity, or love relations) to sketch out new maps for the "self" (NMS 177/263). Thus, Kristeva writes:

> [T]here will be new codes of love in those regions where a new map of the *particular* without property [*"propre" sans propriété*] is being drawn, where new, eternally temporary idealizations (yet indisputable in the present instant) captivate us. This is being talked about on psychoanalytic couches, sought after in those marginal communities that dissent from official morality—children, women, same-sex, and finally heterosexual couples (the most shocking because the most unexpected). (TL 7/16)

Hence, the "transferential or amatory principle," which by its very movement revisits, repeats, and renegotiates the narcissistic structure, "is indispensable for a body to be living rather than a corpse under care" (TL 382). Transference, generator of (self-)love, like Baudelaire's "mystical metamorphosis," "transform[s] error into renewal—remodeling, remaking, reviving a body, a mentality, a life. Or even two" (TL 4/12).

PART III

Derrida: The Mourning of Narcissus

INTRODUCTION: THE VERY CONCEPT OF NARCISSISM

...and of the very concept of narcissism whose aporias are, let us say too quickly and save ourselves a lot of references, the explicit theme of deconstruction.

—*Specters of Marx*

THE DERRIDEAN *COUP*

It is undeniable, as Derrida himself declares in the preceding epigraph from *Specters of Marx*, that deconstruction has always been concerned with the aporetic notion of narcissism; indeed it has been and, as we will maintain in Part III "Derrida: The Mourning of Narcissus," remains its *explicit theme*.[1] Therefore, it is necessary to turn our attention to the books and articles that Derrida devotes to the theme of narcissism. Yet, one searches in vain to find one single text—whether a book, an article, an interview or a film—that explicitly addresses the theme of narcissism.[2] It seems that on this most explicit of themes there is not even one text wholly devoted to it. Of course, it may be countered that there is one published interview, the aptly titled "There is No *One* Narcissism," in which Derrida directly takes up the problems and paradoxes of narcissism.[3] While this is indeed true, the discussion of narcissism, explicit as it may be, takes up a mere page in this nearly twenty-page interview. So, his readers are left wondering what Derrida might have meant when he claimed that the concept of narcissism and its aporias are "the explicit theme of deconstruction." Perhaps one should not interpret the phrase "explicit theme" [*thème explicite*] to mean a theme or topic, like any other, that has been thoroughly treated and elaborated by the author. Rather we would like to suggest that, for Derrida, the aporias of narcissism are integral to the movement of "deconstruction" itself and thus are made "explicit" in each Derridean text.

Let us be more explicit. Since his entrance onto the philosophical scene in the late sixties, Derrida repeatedly and consistently exposed the narcissistic phantasm—the dream of a pure autoaffection and all that it entails (a desire for and hence a tenacious belief in autogenesis, self-presence, immunity, salvation, etc.)—that has fueled Western metaphysics for over two thousand years. In a remarkable reversal of Freud, who portrays the child—"His Majesty the Baby"—as the privileged site of all narcissism (even if it is reborn in parental love), Derrida, in his depictions of the philosopher-father, locates the problem, perhaps even the *source*, of narcissism in the parent rather than child, in the father rather than the son.[4] One only need recall for a moment Derrida's labor in *Dissemination,* one of his earliest (1972) and most well-known texts, to interrupt the auto- and homoerotic relation the philosopher-father has with his offspring, be it a book or a disciple, in our philosophical tradition.[5] While addressing the problem of the foreword in "Outwork, prefacing" ["*Hors Livre, préface*"], Derrida strikes a blow to the narcissism of the author-father:

> As the preface to a book, it is the word of a father assisting and ad-
> miring his work [*la parole du père assistant et admirant*], answering
> for his son, losing his breath in sustaining, retaining, idealizing,
> reinternalizing, and mastering his seed. The scene would be acted
> out, if such were possible, between father and son alone: autoin-
> semination, homoinsemination, reinsemination. Narcissism is the
> law, is on par with the law [*Le narcissisme est la loi, va de pair avec
> elle*]. (D 44–45/53)

In this powerful and satirical portrait of paternal narcissism,
one finds a father, nearly out of breath from his efforts to speak
for, and in the place of, his son. This seemingly loving gesture
of assisting the son is, in Derrida's scenario, an attempt by the
father to master his own seed in order to recuperate any loss
and to ensure a profit. The father's assistance of the son then
aims to guarantee a narcissistic return; that is to say, the father
brings assistance to the son-text so that he may admire himself
reflected in his progeny. Hence narcissism, which "is on par with
the law" or "forms a pair with the law," is for Derrida nothing
other than the law of the father.

In "Passions: 'An Oblique Offering,'" an essay penned over
twenty years after *Dissemination*, Derrida revisits and complicates the problem of parental, or an implied paternal, narcissism
in relation to the name that one bears or gives.[6] His reformula-
tion is as follows:

> The infinite paradoxes of what is so calmly called narcissism are
> outlined here: suppose that X, something or someone (a trace, a
> work, an institution, a child) bears your name, that is to say your
> title. The naïve rendering or common illusion [*fantasme courant*] is
> that you have given your name to X, thus all that returns to X, in a
> direct or indirect way, in a straight or an oblique line, *returns* to
> you, as a profit for your narcissism. (PAS 11–12/31–32)

As Derrida has already demonstrated so persuasively elsewhere,
the name or the title of an individual is detachable from the
person who is its bearer.[7] Thus, this name or title takes on its

own life and is independent from yours. Your name, carried on by a child or a work, "does very well without you or your life" and thus is not dependent upon you as its guarantor (PAS 11/32). By extension, "that which bears, has borne, will bear your name seems sufficiently free, powerful, creative and autonomous to live alone and radically to do without you and your name" (PAS 12/32).[8] In this severance of the name from the father, paternal narcissism finds itself profoundly wounded and hence "frustrated a priori by that which it profits or hopes to profit" (PAS 12/32).

Many readers of Derrida would find themselves quite familiar with this blow that "deconstruction" has dealt the law of (paternal) narcissism that has dominated Western thought.[9] No doubt, many have recognized and remarked upon this Derridean *coup*, which cuts off the king, castrates the father, and even blinds Narcissus. But this is certainly not the whole story, and it would be a mistake to end there. For, to believe that Derrida has single-handedly struck the death blow to narcissism would be not only to underestimate the inexhaustible strategies of narcissism but also to forget that the deconstructive gesture is always double.

Further in the same passage from "Passions," Derrida asks his reader to imagine that your child or X did not want to carry on your name, to continue to be the bearer of your title, and "for one reason or another, X broke free from it and chose himself another name, working a kind of repeated severance of the originary severance [*une sorte de sevrage réitéré du sevrage originaire*]" (PAS 12/32).[10] Derrida claims, somewhat enigmatically, that one's narcissism, now twice wounded, would paradoxically "find itself all the more enriched" (PAS 12/33). He suggests, without elaborating further, that this nonreturn to the name, nonetheless, makes possible an expansion or augmentation of the self: "And thus not to return to itself, which is the condition of the gift (for example, of the name) but also of all expansion of self, of all augmentation of self, of all *auctoritas*" (PAS 12/33).

Thus, Derrida concludes that "[i]n the two cases of this same divided passion" of narcissism it is never possible "to dissociate the greatest profit and the greatest privation," to be capable of calculating with any certainty what one has gained or lost (PAS 12/33). Therefore, no concept of narcissism will be univocal but would be by its very structure aporetic, and any attempt to outline or "construct a non-contradictory or coherent concept of narcissism" must fail (PAS 12/33). Yet, it is this "very concept of narcissism," the paradoxical logic of this divided passion, that Derrida asks us to rethink and even, as we said in the Introduction, to rehabilitate.

PLUS DE NARCISSISME

In "Portrait d'un philosophe: Jacques Derrida," an interview conducted—one could even say "staged"—at the Odéon Theater in Paris, Derrida is faced with an embarrassing question about narcissism, indeed about his *own* narcissism.[11] Before an audience, exposed and vulnerable, Derrida does not attempt to save or redeem himself, to emerge unscathed, safe and sound, from the charge of narcissism. To make matters worse, he not only refuses to deny his own narcissism but also refuses to denounce narcissism in general. What Derrida does denounce, in no uncertain terms, before the eyes of the other, so many others, is the naïve denunciation of narcissism: "In many of my texts," he announces to the audience, "the question of narcissism comes back and I try to denounce precisely the naïveté of denouncing narcissism" (POR 17). Even more boldly in *The Right of Inspection* [*Le droits du regard*], a commentary on a series of photographs by the Belgian photographer Marie-Françoise Plissart, photographs that put into question who is looking and who is being looked at, Derrida calls for, in the strongest of terms, a new way of conceiving of narcissism and even for its eventual rehabilitation. Let us return to the passage with which we began the book:

> One will never have understood anything about the love of the other, of you, of the other as such, you understand [*tu entends bien*],

without a new understanding of narcissism, a new "patience," a
new passion for narcissism. The right to narcissism must be rehabilitated, it needs the time and the means. More narcissism, no
more narcissism. [*Plus de narcissisme.*] Always more narcissism,
never any more narcissism [*Toujours plus de narcissisme*]—clearly
understood, including that of the other. (RI XXVIII)

In a radio interview for France-Culture, Didier Cahen asks
Derrida about his attraction to provocation and, in particular,
his invocation in *The Right of Inspection* for the rehabilitation
of narcissism.[12] When speaking with Cahen, Derrida does not
retract or soften his previous call for a rethinking of narcissism; instead, he denies that there is only *one* narcissism, only
a single form or configuration of narcissism. Rather, Derrida
confounds the traditional distinction between narcissism and
non-narcissism when he claims: "There is not narcissism and
non-narcissism; there are narcissisms that are more or less
comprehensive, generous, open, extended. What is called non-
narcissism is but the economy of a much more welcoming, hos-
pitable narcissism, one that is much more *open to the experience
of the other as other*" (PS 199/212, emphasis mine). Further, in the
same interview, Derrida elaborates: "[T]here are little narcissisms, there are big narcissisms, and there is death in the end,
which is the limit" (PS 199/213).

Clearly Derrida's comments in this interview complicate, if
not undermine, the classical moral opposition between love of
self and love of the other, which one could say found new life
in a certain Freudian articulation of secondary narcissism (for
whom the ego is either emptied out of libido and reinvested in
a love object in an "anaclitic" object-choice or it profits from a
libidinal investment that is wholly turned inward in a "narcissistic" object-choice) and in the work of Emmanuel Levinas (for
whom the figure of Narcissus exemplifies a mortifying self-
enclosure in which the self either cuts itself off from the other
as Other or fully incorporates all alterity into the structures of
the Same).[13] In the light of this long and dominant tradition,

Derrida's invocation to rethink narcissism, or narcissisms, and for its eventual rehabilitation appears nothing short of scandalous. We will thus take seriously Derrida's denunciation of the naïve denunciations of narcissism and will trace his redeployment of the figures of Narcissus and Echo in order to elaborate an ethics of narcissism.

In *Memoires: for Paul de Man* (1988), one of his earliest and most extensive "works of mourning," Derrida declares, clearly in a prescriptive manner,

> On the question of Narcissus and the aforementioned narcissism, it will one day be necessary to read (and I am certain that someone will) those infinitely complicated texts on narcissism; namely, Freud's "On Narcissism: An Introduction," together with all the numerous and inexhaustible texts in which Paul de Man puts Narcissus back in play [*remet Narcisse en scène*]. And if they both were to say that *Narcissus is an allegory*, this should not be taken as a scholarly banality [emphasis mine].[14]

In Part III, it will be our contention that it is Derrida, at least since the 1980s, who has *put Narcissus back on the scene* by reworking the structures of self-relation in terms of the experiences of vision and voice. In order to examine Derrida's "non-naïve" conception of narcissism, we will look to the texts where the figures of Narcissus and Echo show themselves in the Derridean corpus.

One finds that Narcissus appears most frequently in the texts that are concerned with the image or the (self-)portrait, especially the writings that are devoted to drawing, painting, and photography. But perhaps most insistently, Narcissus shows up in Derrida's texts on and of mourning, works written over several decades that are dedicated to the lives and writings of departed friends and are devoted to detailing the structures of mourning at work in each and every death. Thus, in Chapter 5, "The Eye of Narcissus," we will trace Derrida's redeployment of the controversial figure of Narcissus and articulate what is at stake in his rethinking of the structures of narcissism.

More specifically, in our examination of the logic of narcissism at work in Derrida's thought, we will first turn to the paradoxes of the self-portrait, most notably to *Memoirs of the Blind*, as well as to the less well-known, and still untranslated, interview entitled "Portrait d'un philosophe: Jacques Derrida." The discussion of the self-portrait will then open up the question of the aporias of mourning, which, as we shall see, both inaugurate and foreclose any self-relation. In our treatment of Derrida's notion of mourning, we will specifically look to *Memoires: for Paul de Man* and to several essays collected in *The Work of Mourning*, in particular "By Force of Mourning," which takes up the work of Louis Marin on the image. We will also situate Derrida's own discourse on mourning within a psychoanalytic framework by recalling Freud's "Mourning and Melancholia" and Nicholas Abraham and Maria Torok's re-elaboration of this Freudian text. Chapter 5, then, concludes with a mapping out of Derrida's new topology of mourning and an examination of his rethinking of the structures of narcissism, in particular, his Cartesian gloss on Freud: "I mourn, therefore I am."

In Chapter 6, "The Ear of Echo," we will then attempt to articulate the structures and logic of narcissism inscribed as an experience of voice. In the final decade of his life Derrida made frequent, albeit elliptical and often enigmatic, references to Ovid's Echo. Echo appears in diverse places in the Derridean corpus, from *On Touching—Jean-Luc Nancy* and *H. C. for Life, That Is to Say . . .* to *Rogues* and *Derrida* (the movie). We will show how Derrida strategically employs the figure of Echo in order to elucidate a deconstructive notion of the "self" and its relation to the other. We will suggest that in Echo Derrida finds a "little narcissist" who is responsible to the other by answering and returning his call. Yet, while echoing the words of her other, Echo is resourceful enough to speak of and for herself, signing in her own name.

In order to analyze Derrida's novel and powerful interpretation of this seeming powerless figure, we will need to think through Echo's ruse, that is to say, how she circumvents that law (the law that dictates that she will always borrow the other's language) and *invents* a way to reply in her own voice. To understand how Echo is able to manage such a turn of events, it will be necessary to address the complex relationship between iteration and ex-appropriation by examining passages from "'Eating Well,' or the Calculation of the Subject" in *Points . . .* and "Phonographies: Meaning—from Heritage to Horizon" in *Echographies of Television*. Further, so that we may demonstrate that Echo's iteration is not only an appropriation but also a responsible and just response to the call of the other, we will turn to several different texts, including *Monolingualism of the Other; or, The Prosthesis of the Origin* and "Psyche: Inventions of the Other." We will conclude this chapter by arguing that Echo, an exemplary figure of a deconstructive self *and* a figure of deconstruction itself, offers us another narrative of narcissism, which does not disavow mourning but instead opens itself to the experience of the other as other.

CHAPTER 5

The Eye of Narcissus

AN ALLEGORY OF DECONSTRUCTION

An allegorical metonymy [. . .] says something other than what it says and manifests the other [*allos*].

 —*Memoires: for Paul de Man*

It was quite a scene at the grand and historic Odéon Theater in Paris on the evening of February 26, 1996. It was an event unlike any other, yet like so many before and so many after it. Derrida was invited by a group of students and professors from the University of Paris 8 (Vincennes—Saint-Denis) to attend and participate in an evening that was devoted to portraying him in sketches and in speech. Not surprisingly, the events of this singular evening were given the title "Portrait of a Philosopher: Jacques Derrida." The drama at the Odéon unfolded as follows: two actors—one male and one female—read passages from multiple texts by Derrida, including *Memoirs of the Blind*, *Circumfession*, and *Glas*. As Derrida listened to his words pass through the voice of the other, he was observed by the audience as well as by the two artists, one male (Thierry Briault) and one female (Monique Stobienia), who had rendered well over a dozen portraits of him. The series of portraits of Derrida exhibited that evening, surrounding him on the stage, highlighted the strange logic of the self-portrait. While gazing at his own image or, more correctly, images, he was able to see the other seeing him see. To add to the hypernarcissistic nature of the evening, Derrida was not only in attendance, appearing on stage, showing and exposing himself like a blind Narcissus, but also was a respondent, responding to commentaries on his texts and reacting to the portraits sketched of him. One could even say that he assisted or had a hand in creating all these portraits, "all these self-portraits" (POR 8).

To this scene of Derrida *en abyme* and, perhaps more broadly, to the ubiquitous "presence" of Jacques Derrida, the person who showed up at all those conferences, as well as to the image and proper name that is on and in all those books, so many that one can no longer count them, a lone voice, no doubt speaking for so many others, objected. At the Odéon, this voice protested: "What now, they read his texts, they exhibit his portrait 14 or 18 times, you cannot even count how many times [. . .] and what's more he shows up. He appears to participate [*assister*] in all of this. If he were really polite, he would just disappear" (POR 8). This other who speaks, who objects, who looks at and accuses Jacques Derrida of narcissism is the *other* in Derrida, to whom he publicly gave voice on stage, before the gazes of so many. Both at this theater and in his writing, Derrida tries to respond to this voice and this gaze that charge him with narcissism, in other words, that accuse him of indecently showing or exposing himself.

Is it not true that Derrida was making an exhibit of himself or, at the very least, letting himself be put on show, as he had on so many occasions? Jacob Rogozinski, one of the organizers of and participants in the event, who played his part in setting the scene, describes the spectacle as follows: "Jacques Derrida will thus be exposed [*se sera exposé*]. To be heard and understood in all its senses [. . .]. We are showing [*expose*]Jacques

Derrida's portraits, we are showing [*exhibe*] Jacques Derrida off in person, in texts, in paintings. As a result, he ex-poses himself [*s'ex-pose lui-même*], he exposes himself [*s'expose au*] to danger [. . .]" (POR 2).[1] In showing himself to the audience, perhaps in showing off in front of them, even in simply showing up, Rogozinski suggests that Derrida, in exposing himself before the other, every other, is exposed to a certain danger. No doubt Derrida is keenly aware that he is running the risk of getting caught up in this narcissistic scene. One must ask, then, why Derrida would be willing to expose himself to all the dangers that this event would entail and why he would be willing to participate in, as well as witness [*assister à*], such an exhibit of his person, portraits, and work.

In order to begin to address Derrida's defense of his participation on this February evening, one must examine the comments of one of the artists responsible for the portraits on display at the theater and Derrida's reply to them. Thierry Briault suggests to Derrida that one could "read" in all of these portraits a kind of allegory of deconstruction. More specifically, Briault states that in this series of sketches that he and Stobienia rendered one can see "deconstruction" at work in the "allegorized body of Jacques Derrida, the man" ["*corps allégorisé de la personne de Jacques Derrida*"] (POR 5). Derrida admits that he is surprised by the thought that something about his person, whether it be his gestures, voice or gaze, shares an affinity with "deconstruction" (what he calls "*ce nom terrible*") (POR 11). Derrida confesses to those in attendance that he has always had a difficult relationship with his own image, even a kind of allergic reaction to it.[2] Of these uncanny encounters with his own image (especially those of seeing himself on film or in photographs), Derrida says that he does and does not recognize himself, because he sees not only himself but also someone else. Yet, on this occasion, Derrida claims he feels none of his usual embarrassment. He tells Briault that "in all narcissistic simplicity, I feel no discomfort [*gene*] in front of these sketches [. . .]. Therefore you have transfigured me" (POR 11).[3]

Playing on Briault's use of "allegory," Derrida begins to speculate that perhaps his body, his comportment, and the like do speak of "deconstruction" otherwise, because his image, like each image, can function as "an allegorical metonymy." It is necessary to note here that Derrida is not employing "allegory" in the classical or conventional sense of the term, in which a concept or abstract notion (such as "truth") is represented through a figure or person (for example, "woman"). Rather, he hears this word in another way, as *allegoria* (ἀλλος and ἀγορία), or that which speaks otherwise.[4] Whether visual or auditory, whether in images or words, an allegory, as Derrida defines it in the above epigraph from *Memoires: for Paul de Man*, is "something other than what it says and [that which] manifests the other [*allos*]" (MP 37/56).

BLIND NARCISSUS

In order to see himself or show himself, he should only see his two eyes, his own eyes—two eyes that he must get over mourning just as soon, and precisely in order to see himself, eyes that he must just as soon replace [. . .] by other eyes, by eyes that see him, by our eyes.
    —*Memoirs of the Blind*

In Derrida's *Memoirs of the Blind: The Self-Portrait and Other Ruins*, a commentary on a series of drawings chosen by Derrida to be exhibited at the Louvre Museum in an exhibition under the same name, a text on the blindness that lies at the origin of all drawing and visibility and on the destiny of the self-portrait, Derrida invokes the image of Narcissus eleven times.[5] The Narcissus—or perhaps one should say the Narcissi, as there is always more than one—of Derrida's *Memoirs of the Blind* is neither Ovid's nor the Narcissus of the tradition, who is fated to suffer and mourn because his eyes work all too well, because his speculation succeeds. Rather, Derrida's paradoxical Narcissus appears as a blind man who is condemned to mourn the loss of his vision; for this Narcissus will never see himself gazing into his own eyes. Narcissism, like all vision, all drawing, and all self-portraiture is, as Derrida writes, "blinded at the point of 'narcissism,'" that is, "at the very point where it sees itself looking."[6] Narcissus thus suffers from a blind spot, from a "*'punctum caecum,'*" which is "an analogical index of vision itself, of vision in general, of that which, seeing itself see, is nevertheless not reflected, cannot be 'thought' in the specular or speculative mode—and thus is blinded because of this, blinded at the point of 'narcissism'" (MB 53/57). Because of a certain blindness, Derrida's Narcissus suffers from a kind of melancholy, or an impossible mourning, as his desire for totality and sameness is met with only ruins and difference.

However, this blind Narcissus is neither inexorably cut off from any self-relation, from drawing any self-portrait, nor is he trapped in another "narcissism" of the self-same. In *Memoirs of the Blind*, Derrida grafts a new Narcissus onto the sketch in the exhibition entitled "Christ Healing a Blind Man" drawn in the manner of Lucas van Leyde (MB 11/19).[7] The blind man in this drawing, with a bent right arm and extended forefinger, gestures or points toward his blind eyes, in particular to his right one, without ever touching either of them. Without sight and without touch, the blind man sketches his own image for Christ. Derrida interprets this "strange flexion of the arm or reflection of the fold" as "[a] silent auto-affection, a return to oneself, a sort of soul-searching or self-relation without sight or contact" (MB 12/16). Yet, this self-relation or self-return is not pure or complete, for neither the blind man's gaze nor his searching finger make contact with the eye that is seen by the other, that gives itself to visibility.

This blind Narcissus, according to Derrida, invents "a mirror without image"; that is to say, he "lets it be seen that he does not see" ["*donne à voir qu'il ne voit pas*"] (MB 12/18). He does not recuperate his own image, but he does draw himself, he does show himself, he does show up, but to the other. In other words, Derrida's Narcissus shows himself to the other *as* blind. Although any narcissism, like the self-portrait, is by its own logic necessarily blind, or, to put it another way, its vision is never able to coincide with the origin of vision, one can still attempt to reappropriate, to calculate the interest, the benefit, the usury. One can describe it, write it, stage it [*le mettre en scène*]" (MB 70/74).

Derrida's Narcissus may never gaze into his own eyes, but he will attempt to trace his own image in and through the gaze of the other. In showing up on the scene, in showing himself to the other, he can retrace and even attempt to re-appropriate his own image, however ruined it may be. In fact, Derrida claims "that without a movement of narcissistic re-appropriation, the relation to the other would be absolutely destroyed, it would be destroyed in advance. The relation to the other—even if it remains asymmetrical, open, without possible re-appropriation—must trace a movement of re-appropriation in the image of oneself, for example" (PS 199/212).

BLACK NARCISSUS

This finitude can only take that form through the trace of the other in us [. . .]. If there is a finitude of memory, it is because there is something of the other, and of memory as a memory of the other, which comes from the other and comes back to the other [*revient à l'autre*]. It defies any totalization, and directs us to a scene of allegory, to a fiction of prosopopeia, that is, to tropologies of mourning.

    —*Memoires: for Paul de Man*

As melancholy is installed at the heart of the self-portrait, the work of mourning paradoxically involves the impossible yet necessary task of tracing one's own image, of sketching one's self–portrait, in short, of narcissism. In order to get a closer look at this narcissism, this impossible narcissism that is born of mourning, we will turn to a number of Derrida's texts on mourning—in particular, "Mnemosyne" from *Memoires: for Paul de Man* and "By Force of Mourning" in *The Work of Mourning*—that function doubly, as acts of mourning and remembrance for recently departed friends and as treatises on the structures of mourning. In this era of psychoanalysis, Derrida's discourse on mourning must, however obliquely, respond to the terms and tropes used by psychoanalysis, especially those laid out in Freud's well-known essay "Mourning and Melancholia" (1917). Indeed, Derrida's texts on mourning can be read as a reworking and remarking of psychoanalytic discourses, especially those of Freud, Ferenczi, Karl Abraham, Klein, Lacan, and, perhaps most importantly, the highly original work of Nicolas Abraham and Maria Torok. Since a comprehensive examination of the conceptual and terminological rapport between Derrida's writings and those of the above analysts would be a book in itself, I will limit my analysis to only a few tropes that expose Derrida's topology of mourning, which makes any narcissism simultaneously possible *and* impossible.

"[E]ver since psychoanalysis came to mark this discourse," Derrida writes, "the image commonly used to characterize mourning is that of interiorization (an idealizing incorporation, introjection, consumption of the other [...])" (WM 158–59/197). And, Derrida certainly does not abandon the psychoanalytic language of interiorization, including the notions of "incorporation" and "introjection," rather he will remark these terms by inscribing them in another schema. However, before we can sketch out a Derridean configuration of mourning, we must briefly retrace the relationship between mourning and interiorization in the thought of Freud, as well as in the work of Abraham and Torok.

Interiorizing the Other, or the Mourner's Double Bind

I speak of mourning as the attempt, always doomed to fail (thus a constitutive failure, precisely), to incorporate, interiorize, introject, subjectivize the other in me [...]. This is also what I call ex-appropriation, appropriation caught in a double bind: I must and I must not take the other into myself.

—"*Istrice 2: Ick bünn all hier*"

Freud: Mourning and Melancholy

One recalls the well-known distinction that Freud draws between normal mourning and melancholy, or "pathological mourning," in his 1917 essay.[8] First the structural similarities between these two states should be noted: Both mourning and melancholy (1) are reactions to a traumatic loss of someone (a beloved) or something (a place, for example a homeland, or an ideal, such as freedom), (2) involve a painful retreat into the self or the ego, (3) and are marked by a corresponding loss of interest in the outside world, resulting in an inability to libidinally invest in another (i.e., to love). The fundamental difference between these two reactions to loss is the way in which the bereft self retrieves its attachments from the departed love object.

Although the process of mourning is laborious and often lengthy, involving a "great expense of time and cathectic energy" (SE 14:245), it runs its natural course "after a certain lapse of time" (SE 14:244). Yet, how does mourning so efficiently, albeit slowly, accomplish its task? Freud tells his reader that once "reality" has revealed that the love object no longer exists, the mourner will begin to withdraw her libidinal attachments from this object. Although this demand is met with a great deal of opposition or resistance, the reality principle usually gains the upper hand and the work of freeing libido from the lost object begins. In order to withdraw her affective investments, the mourner must paradoxically prolong the "existence" of the object through recollection—drawing up, one by one, memories of the deceased. And, in so doing, the bereaved one "hypercathects" [*überbesetzen*] or intensely invests these memories with libidinal energy. Once the work of remembrance releases libido from the object and it is absorbed back into the ego, "the work of mourning is completed" and, as Freud declares, "the ego becomes free and uninhibited again" (SE 14:245).

In melancholy or pathological mourning, the libido that has been withdrawn from the lost object is not successfully reabsorbed into the ego and is, therefore, not free to be redirected toward another object. Rather, in the case of melancholy, Freud writes: "The ego wants to incorporate the object into itself, and, in accordance with the oral or cannibalistic phase of development in which it is, it wants to do so by devouring it" (SE 14:249–50). Instead of detaching its investments from the object, the ego takes in the abandoned object and forms a narcissistic identification with it, causing a cleavage within the ego itself (which can be witnessed in the frequent "self-reproaches" that are directed at the object now inhabiting the ego or the ego as the lost object). Thus, in melancholy, the self cannot escape the lost object or the relation to the lost object which now haunts it from within.

Abraham and Torok: Introjection and Incorporation

Derrida's own re-elaboration of the structures of mourning is not only indebted to the thought of Freud but also to the inventive and insightful theories of Nicholas Abraham, a Husserlian phenomenologist and practicing analyst, and Maria Torok, a lifelong analyst and researcher. "The alternative topical description they have proposed" of "the Freudian theory of melancholia and mourning"[9] (EO 57) can be found in their 1976 text *The Wolf Man's Magic Word*, for which Derrida wrote the introduction ("Fors: The Anglish Words of Nicolas Abraham and Maria Torok"), and in their 1987 collection of essays entitled *The Shell and the Kernel*.[10] Of their "intervention into Freud," Penelope Deutscher writes, Abraham and Torok do "not dispute the concept of successful mourning, in which libido is successfully detached from the loved other and reabsorbed into the ego. Rather, they add to the concept of successful mourning an expanded concept of the abnormal mourning seen in melancholia, where the subject's ego comes to encrypt [. . .] that lost object."[11]

In their writings Abraham and Torok employ the term "introjection" (this word, "*introjektion*," was first used in a psychoanalytic context by Ferenczi in 1909 and later taken up by Freud, K. Abraham, and Klein) to designate the process of what Freud calls normal mourning. In brief, introjection, for these two analysts, entails the ego reappropriating the drives and desires that it had previously invested in an external object, hence putting an end to its dependency on this object. Following the Freudian distinction between normal and pathological mourning, Abraham and Torok contrast the movement of introjection with that of incorporation. Rather than reabsorbing drives as in the case of introjection, the process of incorporation involves "swallowing" the lost object whole and burying it within the self. In "The Illness of Mourning and the Fantasy of the Exquisite Corpse" (1968), Torok writes: "The incorporated object continues to recall the fact that something else was lost [. . .]. Like a commemorative monument, the incorporated object betokens the place, the date, and the circumstances in which desires were banished from introjection: they stand like tombs in the life of the ego" (SK 114/238). By entombing the lost object in the ego rather than introjecting or reabsorbing libido, the self, although it is "fully bereaved," resists or refuses the work of mourning (SK 127/261). According to Abraham and Torok, "[i]ncorporation is the refusal to reclaim as our own the part of ourselves that we placed in what we lost"; in other words, "incorporation is the refusal to introject the loss" (SK 127/261). Furthermore, in unsuccessful mourning, the self, unable or unwilling to mourn—that is, to fully digest or assimilate its other—incorporates the dead object, which "form[s] a pocket in the mourning body" and "continues to lodge there like something other" (EO 57–58). Abraham and Torok depict this living dead object that is incorporated and buried within the self as a "crypt," which functions both as a monument to a loss and as a form of resistance to this loss.[12]

Derrida: Possible and Impossible Mourning

Derrida, in turn, recasts the Freudian paradigm, in the light of Abraham and Torok's own reworking of notions of mourning and melancholy, as a problem of the "importation of the other in me" (PS 321/331).[13] In Derrida's gloss on Freud's conception of normal mourning, the process of interiorization is portrayed as fundamentally Hegelian: "This is what Hegel calls interiorization which is at the same time memorization—an interiorizing memorization [*Erinnerung*] which is idealizing as well. In the work of mourning, the dead other (it may be an object, an animal, or some other living thing) is taken into me: I kill it and remember it" (EO 58). Thus, the mourner, in taking the lost object into herself (and, here, one finds that Derrida does not maintain the strict distinction that Abraham and Torok insist upon between the interiorization of drives and the internalization of the object) is able to devour, digest, and idealize the dead. Hence, mourning as *Erinnerung* would suggest that the self is able to interiorize the other completely, without remains, and the other (as other) would be no longer.

Conversely, Derrida describes what Freud deems unsuccessful mourning as an incomplete *Erinnerung*, because "this *Erinnerung* goes only so far and then stops" (EO 58); or, in the vocabulary of Abraham and Torok, this process of introjection reaches a limit, a limit that prevents the mourner from fully assimilating the dead. If, as Derrida writes, "I cannot manage to interiorize the dead other," then "I keep it in me, as a persecutor perhaps, a living dead" (EO 58). In this failed *Erinnerung*, "I pretend to keep the dead alive, intact, *safe (save) inside me* [*sauf (fors) en moi*], but it is only in order to refuse, in a necessarily equivocal way, to love the dead as a living part of me, dead *save in me*" (F xvi/17). In this incomplete introjection, this melancholic mourning, the mourner saves the lost object by taking it inside herself and sealing it there. In so doing, in trying to keep the other (in a) safe, she refuses the work of "normal mourning."

In his own recasting of the structures of mourning, Derrida problematizes the hard and fast demarcation between a normal and pathological state to which these analysts so tenaciously adhere. Derrida "suggest[s] that the opposition between incorporation [or melancholy] and introjection [or mourning], however fruitful it may be, remains of limited pertinence" (PS 321/331). The relevance of this demarcation is troubled by Derrida's claim that "[t]here is no successful introjection, [and] there is no pure and simple incorporation" (PS 321/331–32). Further, Derrida writes in "Fors" that "[t]he question—of general appropriation and safekeeping of the other *as other*—can always be raised as the deciding factor, but does it not at the same time

blur the very line it draws between introjection and incorporation, through an irreducible ambiguity?" (F xvii/17).[14] Mourning, for Derrida, can never be an either-or proposition; that is
to say, it is never the case that an individual *either* wholly and
completely absorbs its lost object, thus accomplishing "normal
mourning," *or* entirely refuses the work of mourning by leaving
the beloved other alone (even if this is walled up in a crypt or
safe within the ego).

The blurring of the line between mourning and melancholy,
introjection and incorporation, allows Derrida to put into
question the status of what he calls in "Fors" "so-called normal mourning" (F xvii/17). In speaking of the psychoanalytic
notion of normal mourning in *The Ear of the Other*, Derrida
openly questions "if such a thing exists" (EO 58). Yet, if "normal mourning" does not exist as such, if *Erinnerung* is always
incomplete, then are we to conclude that all mourning becomes melancholic for Derrida? This question would have to be
answered with both a yes and a no. Yes, insofar as the work of
mourning is, in Derridean terms, "the attempt, always doomed
to fail (thus a constitutive failure, precisely), to incorporate, interiorize, introject, subjectivize the other in me" and thus shares
certain structural features with Freud's melancholia (PS 321/331).
No, in so far as Derridean mourning is not a pathological state
that requires a cure, but rather "all mourning" is understood "as
a generalized form of failed mourning" (Deutscher 171).

In *Memoires: for Paul de Man*, Derrida depicts the experience
of mourning as fundamentally aporetic:

> We can only live this experience in the form of an aporia: the aporia
> of mourning and prosopopeia where the possible remains impossi-
> ble. Where *success fails*. And where faithful interiorization bears the
> other and constitutes him in me (in us), at once living and dead. It
> makes the other *part* of us, between us—and then the other no lon-
> ger quite seems to be the other, because we grieve for him and bear
> him *in us*, like an unborn child, like a future. And inversely, the
> *failure succeeds*: an aborted interiorization is at the same time a re-
> spect for the other as other, a sort of tender rejection, a movement

of renunciation which leaves the other alone, outside, over there, in his death, outside of us. (MP 35/54)

In our grief we take the other in, in a certain narcissism, and bear him within us. And in so doing, we cannot avoid denying the otherness of the dead one whom we have loved and are in the throes of mourning. Derrida stresses the failure of what he here describes as "successful" mourning, by showing that any interiorization of the mourned other risks reducing or betraying his absolute alterity. Conversely, a "failed" mourning succeeds, that is to say, what seems to be a failure to mourn, a renunciation of mourning or "an aborted interiorization" that refuses to take the other in and instead leaves him alone in his death, is an act of respect for the other as other.

In another passage from *Memoires*, Derrida further distinguishes the two types of mourning outlined above:

> What does it tell us, this impossible mourning, about an essence of memory? And as concerns the other in us, even in this "distant premonition of the other," where is the most unjust betrayal? Is the most distressing, or even the most deadly infidelity that of a *possible mourning* which would interiorize within us the image, idol, or ideal of the other who is dead and lives only in us? Or is it that of impossible mourning, which, leaving the other his alterity, respecting thus his infinite remove, either refuses to take or is incapable of taking the other within oneself, as in the tomb or the vault of some narcissism [*d'un narcissisme*]? (MP 6/29)

In these often-cited lines from the opening pages of "Mnemosyne," it not only seems that Derrida is contrasting the structures of a "possible" mourning with an "impossible" one, but it also appears as if Derrida were separating these two forms of mourning in exclusively ethical terms—demarcating a just and faithful mourning from a mourning that "is the most unjust betrayal."[15] A possible mourning (like "successful" mourning in the previous passage) would, in an act of infidelity, take the other—the image of the dead other—into oneself and bury it there, "as in the tomb or vault of some narcissism." Conversely an impossible mourning (like the aforementioned "failed" mourning), which involves an inability or a refusal to mourn, would, out of respect for the other as other, not interiorize the dead one but leave him in "his infinite remove."

We must pause for a moment to ask how we are to read the above passages. Is Derrida suggesting, even prescribing, that we ought not mourn as such? More specifically, is he arguing that we ought not remember the other in internalizing memory, "because everything we say or do or cry, however outstretched toward the other we may be, remains *within us*" (PSY 31/20)? Should we read these citations as exhortations to avoid all the traps that narcissism sets for us when we mourn the beloved other? It certainly is tempting to do so, but our reading will resist reducing the complexities of Derrida's thought of mourning to another either/or logic that serves some morality (which must rigidly distinguish a "good" from a "bad" manner of mourning) or to a discourse on health (that will try to cleanly demarcate "normal" from "pathological" mourning). If the Derridean notion of mourning is not a diagnostic tool that allows us to judge the health or illness of an entity, then it must be thought of as "before" or beyond all therapeutics. Although the structures of mourning detailed in Derrida's writing clearly engage with and respond to psychoanalytic discourses, his concern is not that of an analyst, whose interests lay solely with the patient and not with the (dead) other. The analyst depicts mourning and its failures exclusively from the vantage point of the bereaved self, a self that was more or less constituted when the traumatic event befell her. Like a good accountant, the analyst seeks, in an economic manner, what seems to benefit the patient-self. And what appears to profit the mourner is the best method to reclaim for oneself what was previously invested in the lost object, what was originally one's own (SK 127/261). Optimally, in the psychoanalytic narrative, one would get a full return on one's investments or, at the very least, would incur only temporary and minimal losses.

What Freud, along with Abraham and Torok, assume is that the "I" that is traumatized, wounded, even de-centered, by the experience of mourning will reorganize its drives and desires in such a way that trauma is overcome so that the "I" may return to itself more or less intact. For Derrida, mourning involves neither a simple return to oneself (as if the "I" were already constituted prior to the experience of mourning), nor the ability to be done with the other (as if the other's absence reduces my investment in him or his power over me).

Recall that Derrida, in one of the above passages from *Memoires: of Paul de Man*, insists that one "can only live this experience (of mourning) in the form of an aporia." The aporia of mourning thus demands that the mourner "must and must not take the other into [her]self" (PS 321/331). The movement of (re-)appropriation, one could say the work of mourning itself, is "caught in a double bind," as is one's fidelity to the dead other (PS 321/331). In his "dialogue" with Elizabeth Roudinesco, Derrida depicts this double bind as follows:

> Faithfulness prescribes to me at once the necessity and the impossibility of mourning. It enjoins me to take the other within me, to make him live in me, to idealize him, to internalize him, but it also enjoins me to not succeed in the work of mourning: the other must remain the other.[16]

Therefore, fidelity to the (mortal) other, on the one hand, necessitates his appropriation and safekeeping, even though all interiorization deprives him of his otherness. And, on the other the hand, fidelity requires a refusal to appropriate and remember the dead one, a "forgetting" of the other that leaves him utterly alone, abandoned, in his alterity. "The one who has died must of course be forgotten, must be forgotten *well* [*Il faut bien, il faut* bien *oublier le mort*] (WT 160/258).[17] *Both* moments of mourning—each as necessary and inevitable as the other—involve an unavoidable betrayal of the loved one *and* an absolute fidelity to him. Perhaps, we could rephrase the impossible imperative placed on us by mourning as: We must and must not get over the other, making the position of the survivor truly untenable, often unbearable, always impossible.[18]

Another Topology of Mourning

Whatever the truth, alas, of this inevitable interiorization [. . .], this being-in-us reveals a truth *to and at death*, at the moment of death, and even before death, by everything in us that prepares itself for and awaits death, that is, in the undeniable anticipation of mourning [. . .]. It reveals the truth of its topology and tropology.

—*The Work of Mourning*

If the successful interiorization of the other is structurally impossible and if it must not be possible for mourning to succeed, which, in Derridean terms, is for mourning to fail, it is due to another organization of space and visibility—that of looking and being looked at. Was it not Derrida who has made us so keenly aware of the infidelity of which we are capable, even in the most deeply felt mourning, when we "interiorize within us the image, idol, or ideal of the other who is dead and lives only in us?" (MP 6/29). Since "nothing can begin to dissipate the terrifying and chilling light" of the other's death, that "he is no more, he is no longer here, he is no longer there" (WM 160/198), it seems that all that remains of the other are images *in us*, "which might be memories or monuments" (WM 159/198). However, in "By Force of Mourning," Derrida so persuasively argues that "what this rhetoric of space, this topology and tropology, miss [. . .] is that the force of the image has to do less with the fact that one sees something in it than the fact that one is seen there in it. The image sees more than it is seen. The image looks at us" (WM 160/199).

In this essay, which poignantly pays tribute to his close friend and colleague Louis Marin, Derrida says that with Marin (whose work, in particular *Des pouvoirs de l'image*, allows Derrida to refigure the space of interiorization, of the *other in us*, in an altogether different "geometry of gazes [and] orientation of perspectives") he is speaking of images that are not merely seen, but that see, that see us, that look at us, from "within us" (WM 159/198). We not only look at the other, the mortal other, as an image in photographs, on video or in memory, but more important, the departed other looks at us, as Derrida says, *in us*. In speaking of his deceased friend, Derrida declares "I move right before his eyes, and the force of this image is irreversible [. . .]. Louis Marin is looking at me" (WM 160/199). Thus the other, who is no longer, who remains wholly and infinitely other as he was in life and even more so in death, distanced in his infinite alterity, is now an image, but an image that looks at us, *in us*.[19]

How, then, are we to envision this "in us" or "in me" of which Derrida speaks? "When we say 'in us,'" Derrida writes, "we speak so easily and so painfully of inside and outside, we are naming space" (WM 159/198). But, what sort of interior and exterior spaces is he sketching out? Is not the language of inside and outside a problematic and overdetermined remnant of the long, egocentric history of subjectivity? Derrida insists that the topology that he is tracing is "something completely other than a mere subjective interiority, [rather it is] a place open to an infinite transcendence" (WM 161/200). It is precisely this gaze of the mortal other—which I bear in me and which bears on me—that cannot be fully appropriated by any interiority.[20] The gaze of the other remains infinitely other and will remain the other's: No narcissism can wholly incorporate it and no subjective speculation can reduce its singular force.

Therefore, this being "in us" should not be thought of as a purely interior speculation or as "narcissism" as it has been traditionally understood. For this inversion and dissymmetry of the gaze can only be internalized by wounding, fracturing, and exceeding the interiority that welcomes it in love and hospitality. The living are "obliged to harbor something that is greater and other than them; *something outside them within them*" (MP 34/54). Thus, any being "in us" of the mortal other cannot be conceived, in Derridean terms, as "the simple inclusion of a narcissistic fantasy in a subjectivity that is closed upon itself or even identical to itself" (MP 22/44). Rather, it is Derrida's contention that the logic of narcissism is far too complex and too circuitous to be equated with any simple speculation or classical form of subjectivity, since narcissism, even armed with all its tricks, is unable to reduce the other, whether dead or alive, to the structures of the same.

"I Mourn Therefore I Am," or an Im-possible Narcissism

I mourn therefore I am, I am—dead with the death of the other, my relation to myself is first of all plunged into mourning, a mourning that is moreover impossible.

    —*"Istrice 2: Ick bünn all hier"*

Derrida writes that "at the instant of [the other's] death, the limit of narcissistic reappropriation becomes terribly sharp," and hence the "narcissistic wound enlarges infinitely for want of being able to be narcissistic any longer, for no longer even finding appeasement in that *Erinnerung* we call the work of mourning" (PSY 31/21). Yet, Derrida also claims that "[b]ecause the other, over there, remains irreducible, because he resists all interiorization, subjectification, idealization in a work of mourning, the ruse of narcissism never comes to an end" (MB 70/74). Thus, narcissism remains a kind of speculation, one with infinite strategies, even though this speculation can only "succeed in supposing the other" and, in supposing the other, all *autonomy* will be abandoned in advance (MP 32/52). Derrida outlines this paradoxical logic of narcissism as follows: "[I]t is only starting from the other, from a kind of self-renunciation, that narcissism grows, and grows always in losing itself, and this contradiction is at once its limit and condition" (POR 17). It is precisely with the death of the other, when my power to reappropriate is most limited, that narcissism "grows" and, as such, becomes *my* narcissism.

In sketching out how mourning constitutes narcissism, we must not forget that Derrida defines "mourning" more broadly than the analysts, who generally employ the term to designate a psychical response to an "actual" death of a loved one. All mourning, in Derrida's schema, however, belongs to "originary mourning," which does not take place at any particular moment and is not the direct result of any particular death, but is "the inscription of the mortal other [alive or dead] in me" (POR 16). If originary mourning is the structural possibility of the other's death (as well as my own), then it need not wait for the other to die for its work to begin. Simply put: "This 'mourning effect' thus does not wait for death" (WT 160/258). Since the other's mortality is inscribed in me prior to his "real" death, I begin mourning him long before his departure from this world. And, as we saw in the preceding sections, mourning entails bearing the other *in me* whose gaze bears on me. Therefore, Derrida writes, "[t]his carrying of the mortal other 'in me outside me' instructs or institutes my 'self' and my relation to 'myself' already before the death of the other" (PS 321/331).

Any "me" or "us" can only come to be, then, by virtue of "the other as the other who can die, leaving in me or in us this memory of the other" (MP 33/52–53). Nonetheless, Derrida writes, "[e]ven if this metonymy of the other in ourselves already constituted the truth and the possibility of our relation to the living other, death brings it out into more abundant light" (PSY 31/20–21). The loss of the other to death radically affects my relation to myself, which is "first of all plunged into mourning, a mourning that is moreover impossible [*mon rapport à moi est d'abord endeuillé, d'un deuil d'ailleurs impossible*]"—impossible because "I am—dead with the death of the other [*je suis—mort de la mort de l'autre*]" (PS 321/331).[21] Because the other's death interrupts and exceeds my "interiority," because it deprives me of all autonomy (by short-circuiting my powers of recuperation), "I" am—*dead* with the dead other. Yet, as I mourn the loss of the other (and, no less, the interruption of the phantasm of my autonomy), "I" *am*—dead with the other's death. It is the undeniable and irrevocable absence of the other—"[t]his terrible solitude which is mine or ours at the death of the

other" that "constitutes that relationship to the self which we call
'me,' 'us,' 'between us,' 'subjectivity,' intersubjectivity,' 'memory'"
(MP 33/52–53). It is the death of the other, for Derrida, that
"makes manifest the limits of a *me* or an *us*" (MP 34/53–54).

Unlike the psychoanalytic discourses on mourning where
an established ego or the identity of the "I" precedes, and consequently can be destabilized by, the ordeal of mourning, Derrida's mourning inaugurates a self. In this light, I would like to
suggest that we should not read Derrida's gloss—"I mourn
therefore I am [*je suis endeuillé donc je suis*]"—on Descartes's
famous phrase as pastiche, but as a "first principle" of a Derridean philosophy of the "self" (whether it be referred to as the "I"
[*je*], "me" [*moi*], ego, *chez soi*, autos, *ipse*, etc.) (PS 321/331). Indeed what Derrida, in the manner of Levinas, calls the *ipse* or
ipseity, that is, a certain power or mastery that first begins with
a "*je peux*" ("I can" or "I am able to") and thus the ability to
welcome the other into one's home, into the *chez soi*, and to offer hospitality, is itself constituted by "first" being subject to an
originary mourning. Only by virtue of the ordeal of mourning
can any singularity emerge. It is only in and through the inscription of the mortal other *in* the *ipse*, and consequently as a
result of its own lack of mastery, that it is able to appear to itself (POR 16).[22] Thus, from the inscription of the mortal other
in us, from this site of mourning, narcissism manifests itself.

Let us return for a moment to the strange space of images
and gazes that is marked by "an *absolute* excess and dissymmetry in the space of what relates us to ourselves" (WM 161/200).
In bereavement, the other in looking at us and regarding us, *in
us*, relates us to ourselves. Because before I can appear to myself
as singular, as a self, I must appear before the mortal other. In
"By Force of Mourning," Derrida sketches out this logic in
terms of his own friendship with Marin. Derrida confesses that
he feels Marin's gaze upon him and admits that "[i]n relationship to myself, he is here in me before me, stronger and more
forceful than I" (WM 160/199). It is before the gaze of the
other—this entirely singular gaze—that I (can) *appear*. Of

Marin, Derrida says "*I appear* before him, before his word and gaze," and "[h]e is my law, the law" (WM 160/199, my emphasis). It is in this inverted interiority where I am looked at but am blind by situation, where I know that I am an image for the other who remains irreducible, that "I can say *cogito, sum*" (WM 160/199). Derrida depicts this relation to oneself as a Narcissus "who gazes at himself only from the gaze of the other" (WM 164/204). Thus, he writes, "[t]he *Selbst*, the *soi-même*, the self appears to itself only in this bereaved allegory, in this hallucinatory prosopopeia" (MP 28–29/49). Derrida's blind Narcissus must continue to mourn and is born only from his mourning, as his autonomy and his vision are not and will never be his but are always a gift from the other.

ASSISTING NARCISSUS

I said to myself that perhaps the least inadequate word to describe what I am doing here among you, in front of you, but among you, in the midst of you, is the word assistant. Assistant.

—"Portrait d'un philosophe: Jacques Derrida"

Let us revisit the Odéon, where on center stage in front of the gaze of so many others Derrida attempted to answer the charge of narcissism. On this stage and in his writings, he offered a defense, perhaps an apology, not only for narcissism in general, but also for his own appearing on the scene—for showing up at and participating in innumerable conferences, interviews, photographs, films, and even for authoring so many texts.[23] Derrida claimed before the audience that his appearance on this particular evening, which was like so many other occasions, was not motivated by his desire to appear a little more but rather by his hope that he may disappear a little more. As Derrida's "presence" was diminished, not increased, by these fourteen or eighteen portraits, his numerous appearances, he contended, decreased the effects of his authority, because "[t]hat which, on this stage, plupresently, proffers itself in the present, so as to deconstruct the 'illusion' or 'error' of the present will be named the 'attending discourse' [*discours d'assistance*]" (D 324/360). At this theater, Derrida announced that as long as he is still among the living his absence from the scene would be more authoritarian and violent by investing his image and proper name with a power and force that only absence and death can confer upon a corpus. Thus, by appearing, by attending, by participating, Derrida hoped to attenuate the effects of authority and mastery.

Derrida's defense for his showing up at the Odéon Theater, he suggested, could be summed up in a single word—*assistant*. No doubt, those familiar with Derrida's early work, in particular, *Dissemination*, would find this appeal to the terms *assistant* and *assistance* somewhat suspect or, to say the least, confusing.[24] Recall the scathing portrait of the philosopher-father (treated in the introduction to Part III), who must forever bring assistance in the form of living speech to his writing, the (bastard) son, lest the meaning of his words be misinterpreted. Remember that "the word of a father assisting and admiring [*la parole du père assistant et admirant*] his work, answering for his son" was described by Derrida as the father's desperate attempt to master his progeny (D 44–45/52–53).

We would like to suggest that Derrida reinscribes this term by exploiting the various resonances of the French noun *l'assistant* and the verb *assister (à)* in both the transitive and intransitive forms, so that it may be heard otherwise. For most of Derrida's professional life he bore the title *maître-assistant*, a title he found very appropriate. Of the two terms in this title, he privileged *assistant* rather than *maître* or master and interprets this title to mean one who "assists." "*Assister à*," the intransitive form of the verb, designates in its most common usage to attend or be present as a spectator or witness at an event, like at a public lecture or a tennis match; it also can mean to participate or take part in a gathering. The transitive from of the French "*assister*" functions more like the English verb "to assist," meaning to aid or accompany someone in his or her work or, more colloquially, to lend someone a hand. It can also designate the act of aiding, caring for, or giving protection to another; for example, to the sick or the dying. By linking the various senses of this word—attending, appearing, and participating, which all share a sense of showing oneself to the other, with lending assistance to the other in his travail—Derrida thus re-marks his own use of this term and, in so doing, reduces the effects of (his own) mastery. One could then portray Derrida's frequent appearances on the intellectual scene—as he portrays van Leyde's blind man—as a blind Narcissus, a narcissist nonetheless, who "shows himself, [who] shows up, but to the *other*" [*Il se montre lui-même, mais à l'autre*] (MB 12/18, italics my own).

CHAPTER 6

The Ear of Echo

It must be confessed that the self is nothing more than an echo.
   —Paul Valéry, *Cahiers*

THE SUBJECT OF ECHO

In the 1989 interview with Jean-Luc Nancy, "'Eating Well,' or the Calculation of the Subject," Derrida suggests that it would be possible

> to reconstruct a discourse around a subject that would not be pre-deconstructive, around a subject that would no longer include a figure of mastery of self, of adequation to self, center and origin of the world [. . .], but which would define the subject rather as a finite experience of non-identity to self, as the underivable interpellation insomuch as it comes from the other, from the trace of the other, with all the paradoxes or the aporia of being-before-the-law. (PS 266/280)

If one were to attempt such a feat—to reconstruct a non-pre-deconstructive discourse about the "subject"—it would first be necessary to return to the scene where the "self," the "*ipse*," the "I" is inaugurated.[1] As was demonstrated in the previous chapter, Derrida locates the coming to be of any "self" within the paradoxical logic of narcissism, which is inextricably bound up with an experience of mourning. Derrida's Narcissus, condemned as he is to blindness, must mourn not only the other whom he can never wholly appropriate but also his own autonomy. Yet, like a blind man feeling his way in the dark, he will ceaselessly attempt to sketch his own portrait, to trace his own image. And, even though each gesture of narcissistic reappropriation is destined to fail, such gestures should be attempted, time and again, if there is to be any relation to the other, any love, any hospitality.

"The all-powerful logic of narcissism [*la toute puissance du narcissisme*]" that is staged and enacted as an "experience of the gaze" finds a parallel in the experience of voice in the figure of Echo.[2] On the final page of "By Force of Mourning," Derrida links the gaze with voice, Narcissus with Echo, as two modes of and two names for self-relation. "One knows," Derrida writes, "that the relation to oneself, that Narcissus himself, gazes at himself only from the gaze of the other, and precedes himself, answering only for himself, only from the resonance of Echo" (WM 164/204). If Narcissus is to hear himself speak, if he is to answer for himself, ironically he will have to do so through the resonance of Echo. Before we can speak of Narcissus and his voice, it is necessary to listen closely to Derrida's allegory of Echo.

Since the appearance of Ovid's *Metamorphoses*, Echo has been heard incessantly miming, repeating, and sending back the words of Narcissus. And, with insistence, Derrida returns to the famous scene between Narcissus and Echo, repeating their story, time and again, as if he will say something new by echoing the poet's words. As we recall, Echo was condemned by divine interdiction to reduplicate only a deformed or deficient discourse of the same. Thus it can be argued that Echo is nothing but "voice" but has no voice of her own, that she is simply a reflecting surface for Narcissus yet has no image herself. Echo, perhaps the paradigmatic figure of "woman," is but a mere resonance of man and seems to be truly an impossible figure. Why, then, does Derrida in a number of his later texts and interviews—most notably in *Rogues: Two Essays on Reason, On Touching—Jean-Luc Nancy, The Work of Mourning*,

Prégnances: Lavis de Colette Deblé, as well as in the movie *Derrida*—recall and call upon the figure of Echo?[3] We will give Derrida's rereading of the figure of Echo a fair hearing and, in listening to Derrida recount Echo's story, will attempt to allow her to speak again and otherwise. And, in once again revisiting Ovid's myth of Echo and Narcissus, we will try to articulate a Derridean notion of the "self," while remaining mindful that "if one wants to reconstruct a concept of the subject 'after deconstruction,' [. . .] one has to shape a logic and a topic that are rather powerful, supple, articulated, and that therefore can be disarticulated" (PS 321/331–32). Thus, we will attempt to demonstrate that in Derrida's figure of Echo one finds such a supple logic and topic of the "subject," one that can be articulated and disarticulated. In order to do this, one must journey through an exploration of voice as a process of iteration and ex-appropriation, which must always take the form of, and gain its force from, a loving affirmation.

GIVING ECHO ANOTHER HEARING

This voice lets itself be heard (*se donne à entendre*), and it speaks otherwise [. . .].
   —"Voice II"

When retelling this all-too-well-known myth, Derrida stresses Echo's singular condition—having been punished by a jealous goddess, she is bound by a divine prohibition that deprives her of the ability to initiate speech. This inescapable "sovereign in-junction," which marks Echo's situation, is her law (R xii/10). This law also dictates that when Echo hears the words of others she will be unable to hold her tongue and remain silent. Thus, she will be compelled to repeat the final words or syllables that fall upon her ears. It would not be surprising, then, if one were to depict Echo as eternally trapped by the divine law that has condemned her, like Sisyphus, to an absurd repetition. Echo most certainly seems to be caught inexorably within an *aporia*, from which there appears to be no way out.

Derrida's Echo is bound by the law—a law that dictates that she may speak only after the other, "for the other will have spoken first" (MP 37/56). Although she will forever follow the other, Derrida finds possibilities in this im-possible figure. He even suggests that Echo is perhaps not as naïve as she seems and that, in fact, she may have discovered a clever *poros* or passage to escape her *aporia*.[4] In Derrida's interpretation of this scene, Echo finds a way to circumvent the sovereign injunction and thus to foil the tyranny of the law. Although she "seems" to be complying with the law that has condemned her to mere repetition, Echo is, according to Derrida, only "pretending" to do so. He describes her duplicity when he writes that Echo is "the voice of another who *feigns* to send back to Narcissus the end of his sentences" (POR 16–17, emphasis mine). In *On Touching—Jean-Luc Nancy*, Derrida, posing as Narcissus, identifies with Echo when, speaking in a direct address, he confesses his own deception to her: "[Y]ou, my Echo, [. . .] you ruse, as do I, with the divine interdiction, [. . .] you deceive it in order to speak [. . .] while pretending to repeat the end of my sentences" (OT 291/327). Perhaps Derrida's reading of Echo's ruse, which itself entails a fair share of *mêtis* or cunning intelligence, will allow us to hear the following words by Ovid anew: Echo "waits for what her state permits: to catch the sounds that she can give back with her own voice" (Ovid 92).

ECHO'S RUSE

One recalls [. . .] the ruse of the sublime Echo.

    —*Prégnances*

So that we may better understand Echo's ruse—that is, how she outsmarts the law by letting be heard "something other than what she seems to be saying" so that she may speak "[o]f herself and on her own"—it is necessary for us to first focus our attention on the relationship between iteration and (ex-)appropriation (R xii/11). Due to her unique state, which has deprived her of a "voice" as it would be classically understood, seemingly leaving her without the ability to speak of and for herself, indeed, to speak as a self, Echo must contrive to appropriate what she does not have. We will thus see that when Echo appears to be merely miming Narcissus, she is in fact attempting the im-possible—to appropriate the unappropriable, the foreign, the transcendent, the absolutely or wholly other.

But, before we rush too far ahead, it is necessary to backtrack a little and patiently retrace Echo's steps. We know from Ovid that "[w]hen Echo saw Narcissus roaming through the lonely fields, she was inflamed with love, and—furtively—she followed in his footsteps" (Ovid 92). Yet, she remained bound by an infernal silence. One day as Echo was tracking her love-object, Narcissus, separated from his companions, called out: "Is anyone nearby?" Echo's opportunity had finally arrived, and she joyfully replied by echoing "Nearby." It almost seems that Echo "knew" that by reiterating Narcissus's phrases, by allowing his words and sounds to pass through her mouth, she would be able to draw him nearer to her, begin to identify with him, and ultimately respond to her beloved by appropriating his locutions for herself.

Derrida could be speaking of Echo's situation in *Echographies of Television* when he declares that "even if only virtually, I must be able by virtue of this iterability to appropriate: to see what I see, to get closer, to begin to identify, to recognize, in the broadest sense of these terms—these are all processes of appropriation."[5] Further, in the same text, Derrida calls this "process of appropriation by repetition, by identification, by idealization [in which] I appropriate the other or an object" *intentionality* (E 111/124). If one were to condense the logic of these two statements, it would be necessary to conclude that iteration is indispensable for any form of appropriation (which makes perception, identification, and meaning possible) and that all these forms of appropriation are, for Derrida, a kind of intentionality. It seems, then, that while feigning to reproduce the end of Narcissus's sentences, Echo "intends"—if intentionality is defined as, and I repeat, "a process of appropriation by

repetition, by identification, by idealization"—to speak for herself and to declare her love.

ECHO EATS WELL

[I]f, in the (symbolic or real) experience of the "eat-speak-interiorize," the
ethical frontier no longer rigorously passes between the "Thou shalt not kill"
(man, thy neighbor) and the "Thou shalt not put to death the living in general," but rather between several infinitely different modes of the conception-
appropriation-assimilation of the other, then as concerns the "Good" of every
morality, the question will come back to determining the best, most respectful, most grateful, and also most giving way of relating to the other and relating the other to the self.
    —"Eating Well"

In order to more fully understand how Echo's iteration appropriates, we will need to rehearse a few lessons from the
text with which we opened this chapter—"'Eating Well' or the
Calculation of the Subject." So that Echo may truly speak for
herself, so that she may reply to her other while reduplicating
his words, she must first (if one can truly speak here of any
logical or temporal priority) take in the sounds that are destined for her ears. More generally, if Echo is to take up her
other, she will have to *take him in*. If, as Derrida maintains,
"everything that happens at the edge of the orifices (of orality,
but also of the ear, the eye—and all the 'senses' in general) the
metonymy of 'eating well' [*bien manger*] would always be the
rule," then Echo will have to incorporate her other (PS 282/296).
Eating, Derrida insists, is not an option: "One eats [the other]
regardless and lets oneself be eaten by him" (PS 282/296). Of
course, we should hear this Derridean declaration as extending
far beyond any empirical consumption of food or drink to "the
very concept of experience" itself (PS 283/297), because the law
of need or desire—the "'it is necessary [*il faut*]' that I want the
thing to be mine"—is equally at work in all experience, from
eating and perceiving to loving and mourning (E 111/124).[6]

If one must "eat," if incorporation is inescapable for a finite being, then the question should be posed: "How is this metonymy of introjection to be regulated?" (PS 282/296). Rather than turning to questions concerning what one should eat or what tastes good to eat (however fruitful they may be), we will direct our attention to *how* one ought to eat (the other). For Derrida, the truly ethical dilemma is determining the most generous, respectful, and grateful way of relating to the other who "is to be assimilated, interiorized, understood ideally" (PS 283/297). Truly eating well, in his estimation, would never be reducible to "taking in and grasping in itself" but rather would require an identification with the other who will be consumed (PS 282/296–97). Such an "identifying appropriation" can only take place on the condition that one addresses oneself to the other—if one "speak[s] to him or her in words that also pass through the mouth, the ear, and sight" (PS 283/297). And, in addressing oneself to the other, one learns "to-give-the-other-to-eat," because one offers up words to the other, words that he, in turn, will consume with his eyes, ears, and mouth. Derrida reminds us that "[o]ne never eats entirely on one's own," and "this constitutes the rule and the underlying statement, 'One must eat well,' [. . .] a rule offering infinite hospitality" (PS 282/297). In love and hospitality, Echo will eat Narcissus and give Narcissus to eat.

Therefore, such an address to the other would involve, as Derrida argues in *Memoires: for Paul de Man*, "a movement in which an interiorizing idealization takes in itself or upon itself the body and voice of the other, the other's visage and person" (MP 34/53). Derrida insists that "[t]his mimetic interiorization is not fictive," for any identificatory iteration "takes place in a body" (MP 34/53).[7] For, it is with her ears and her mouth that Echo both quasi-literally and ideally ingests the words of Narcissus. Although Derrida claims that the interiorization of the other must "take place in a voice and a body as such," this idealizing appropriation also produces or "makes a place for a body, a voice, and a soul which, although 'ours,' did not exist and had no meaning *before* this possibility that one *must* always begin by remembering, and whose trace must be followed" (MP 34–35/53–54). One could therefore justifiably conclude that this "mimetic interiorization," which always takes place in a corporeal being, is what gives birth to a singular or unique body, voice, soul, etc.

An analogy can thus be drawn between the introjection of the other's gaze (as in the case of Narcissus), which bears on us "in us," and the interiorization of the voice of the other (as in the case of Echo). In each experience, we find ourselves *before* the other (as before the law), who will have always come *before* us. Thus, to eat (the other) well, with eye, ear, or mouth, would not only involve an identification with the other by repeating his words but also require respect for the voice or the gaze of the other, which, as our law, "is *in us* who are *before it*" (PS 283/297). Moreover, the other, who is taken up and appropriated, not only precedes but also exceeds us by "resist[ing] all subjectivation, even to the point of the interiorization-idealization of what one calls the work of mourning" (PS 270–71/285). As we saw in the preceding chapter, Derrida shows in his works of morning that no appropriation or re-appropriation (incorporation, introjection, idealization) can ever be complete or "successful." Therefore, any attempt to appropriate the other "is, in advance, held in check or threatened by failure, virtually forbidden, limited, finite" (E 111/123).

Yet, according to Derrida, although the absolute alterity of the other, time and again, thwarts or bars our attempts at appropriation and hence limits our insatiable desires, this is what we desire. Whether we are conscious of it or not, he contends, we "desire" that the other "remain foreign, transcendent, other" (E 111/124). Indeed, for there to be desire at all, for there to be love, it is essential that the other remain sufficiently other so that one still has an interest in making it one's own.

Derrida reiterates: "[r]eappropriation always takes place."[8] And this process of re-appropriation is perhaps intrinsic to the movement of life itself, for it begins "at 'birth,' and possibly even

prior to it," and thus precedes any "subject," any "I," or any consciousness (PS 270/285).[9] Further, each and every movement of
appropriation is, in effect, an "ex-appropriation" or a "finite appropriation" (E 111/124). In *Echographies of Television*, Derrida
describes the movement of ex-appropriation as double: It involves both an inescapable gesture of (re-)appropriation and
the necessary failure to interiorize that which remains outside,
over there, always out of reach.[10] The double movement of ex-
appropriation thus prevents the self from closing itself off from
the other or from entirely enclosing the other within the self.
In fact, ex-appropriation, for Derrida, "implies the irreducibil-
ity of the relation to the other" (PS 270/285).

ECHO'S CALL "TO COME"

If I seem to be insisting a bit too much on these *Metamorphoses*, it is because
everything in this famous scene turns around a call *to come*.
    —*Rogues*

As he reveals in the above passage cited from *Rogues*, Derrida
returns to the exchange between Narcissus and Echo in the
Metamorphoses, once again, one more time, once and for all. He
insists on returning to this scene because it pivots around "a call
to come [*un appel à venir*]" (R xii/10). Of course, Derrida is referring here to the moment in Ovid's text when Narcissus beck-
ons Echo to come, to which Echo responds by returning his
call. Of Narcissus, Ovid writes: "And, stupefied, he looks around
and shouts: 'Come! Come!',", and, in turn, in taking her turn,
Echo "calls out, 'Come! Come!' to him who called" (Ovid 92).
Although Echo seems simply to repeat the call of Narcissus,
without simulacrum, Derrida contends that "another simulacrum slips in to make her response something more than a
mere reiteration" (R xii/10).[11] In *Prégnances*, a text of praise for
the paintings of Colette Deblé, Derrida portrays Echo as quite
skillful at language play. Both subtly and ingeniously, Echo

pretends to cite Narcissus verbatim in order to allow his words to resonate otherwise, making it possible to hear this call *to come* anew.

In Derrida's ear, Echo's repetition of this call to come—a call that is itself originally doubled—sounds like an entirely new sentence: "She says in an inaugural fashion, she declares her love, and calls for the first time, all the while repeating the 'Come!' of Narcissus, all the while echoing narcissistic words" (R xii/10). Echo's reply, Derrida writes, is a "repeated fragment [that becomes] another sentence, invented, original" (POR 15–16). Therefore, what Derrida hears in Echo's reply to Narcissus is by no means an empty reduplication or a hollow reverberation of the same, but a unique and inventive response. Nonetheless, Echo's invention, like any invention, cannot dispense with the conventions of the past and is thus never "foreign to repetition and memory" (PSY 61/61). Rather, to open oneself, as Echo so passionately does, to the future, to what is to come, it is necessary to pass "through the economy of the same, indeed while miming or repeating it" (PSY 60/60). It is precisely "at the intersection of repetition and the unforeseeable" that one cannot "see *coming* what remains *to come*" (R xii/10–11).

And, what of this call to come that can be heard echoing at the *intersection of repetition and the unforeseeable*? In *Monolingualism of the Other*, Derrida speaks of this call, this appeal, *to come [appel à venir]*, which is *first* issued by the other. The call to come—which welcomes and gathers language together in its uniqueness or singularity, which promises a language or an idiom—is always coming from the other, and to it one can only respond.[12] In "Eating Well," Derrida adds that "to this call I can only answer, have already answered, even if I think that I am answering 'no'" (PS 261/276). Thus, it is inevitable that Echo will answer the call of Narcissus. Yet, what would a just reply to this appeal from the other sound like?

Although Echo is bound by her condition to return Narcissus's call to come, Derrida emphasizes that she lovingly and lucidly "take[s] back the initiative of answering or responding in a responsible way" (R xi–xii/10). Having recognized that she does not possess the power to issue a call to the other (which is always an appeal for the other *to come*) and that she is thus incapable of making him come, Echo does what it is in her power to do—she prepares for and anticipates his arrival. Indeed, it is Echo who knows better than anyone that "one does not make the other come," but that "one lets him come by preparing for his coming" (PSY 60/60). As resourceful as she may be, Echo realizes that "the other is what is never inventible" (PSY 62/61). And "if the other is precisely what is not invented," then any "initiative or deconstructive inventiveness" on Echo's part would "consist only in opening, in uncloseting, destabilizing foreclusionary structures so as to allow for the passage to the other" (PSY 60/60).

Echo's deconstructive inventiveness then can be heard reverberating in her reply—"'Come! Come!' to him who called"—a response that Derrida portrays as both responsible and affirmative. Echo affirms Narcissus's call by returning it in a way that her words are at once an answer and an invitation. "In repeating, she responds to him. In repeating, she corresponds with him" (DM). Echo's "response with another 'come' seems to be," Derrida insists, "the only invention that is desirable and worthy of interest" (PSY 61/60). This seemingly simple reply acknowledges and accepts that the other has always come before me and that I am forever speaking the other's language, borrowing it from him in order to speak to him. Therefore, the language that Echo speaks not only comes from her other but is also destined for him; "and, since, it returns to the other, it exists asymmetrically, always for the other, from the other, kept by the other" (MO 40/70). Knowing full well that she "has no choice but to let the other speak, since [she] cannot make the other speak without the other having *already* spoken," Echo "speaks the other and makes the other speak" (MP 37–38/56). But Echo also follows this trace of the other's language, so that she may speak in allegory, in other words, so that her "speech always say[s] something other than what it says" (MP 37–38/56).

SIGNED ECHO

[. . .] in her own name signed Echo.

   —*Prégnances*

Signature

While wholly affirming the precedence and the alterity of the other, which necessarily entails a mourning of her autonomy (a lesson which is impossible for Ovid's Narcissus to come to terms with, hence his morbid solution), "Echo, in her loving and infinite cleverness, arranges it so that in repeating the last syllables of the words of Narcissus, she speaks in such a way that the words become her own" (DM). In speaking his language, in identifying with and interiorizing Narcissus, in sending his words back to him, Echo, Derrida contends, appropriates something of the other—his language or idiom—for herself. And in this "spectacular [. . .] scene [. . .] when Echo traps Narcissus in a certain way," Echo ruses to appropriate something of Narcissus so that she may appropriate her*self* (DM, emphasis mine). It is "first and foremost 'myself,' the 'I' itself," argues Derrida, "which must also be appropriated by an appropriating *ipse*, whose 'power'[. . .] does not yet have the form of egohood, much less that of consciousness" (E 111/124).[13]

   But, it is in "Veni," the preface to *Rogues*, where Derrida fully reveals Echo's ruse—that is, how in speaking (through) the other she speaks freely for herself. In echoing the other, Echo speaks "[o]f herself and on her own" (R xii/11). Put otherwise, Derrida insists, as he does in every reference he has made to this infamous exchange, that Echo "feign[s] to repeat [. . .] in order to sign in that very instant in her *own name*" (R xi/10, emphasis mine). Yet, one may still wonder what allows Echo's repetition to escape the fate of mere repetition or reduplication to become a unique signature. The answer may be found in the following passage from "Veni": Echo speaks "in an inaugural fashion, she declares her love, and calls for the first time, all the while repeating the 'Come!' of Narcissus, all the while echoing narcissistic words" (R xii/10). Echo not only speaks in her *own name* but also *declares her love*. How are we to understand this relationship between Echo's signature and her avowal of love? Is this mere rhetorical flourish on Derrida's part, or does "love" play a more fundamental role in the allegory of Echo, who is perhaps not simply a figure of a deconstructive self but also an exemplary figure for deconstruction itself?

In Derrida's gloss of Ovid's tale, which he says "is a love story, after all" (DM), it is Echo's love that infuses and gives new life to the words of Narcissus; it is her love that exceeds his call *to come*: "She overflows with love; her love overflows the calls of Narcissus" (R xii/10). Briefly, we turn to Peggy Kamuf's inspired chapter "Deconstruction and Love" from her *Book of Addresses* in order to better understand why and "how a loving movement is the indispensable key to understanding what deconstruction [i.e., Echo] does."[14] In this chapter, Kamuf analyzes Derrida's own public pronouncement of love in a 1979 round-table discussion: "I love very much everything that I deconstruct in my own manner; the texts I want to read from the deconstructive point of view are texts that I love" (EO 87). Her interpretation of Derrida's declared love of texts, texts that he "deconstructs" precisely because he feels an "impulse of identification" and "loving jealousy" toward them, could be applied to our analysis of the allegory of Echo.

Kamuf shows that a deconstructive reading, which always replies to a call from the other, is never reducible to a mere technical operation that is neutral (or negative), and is thus not "performed by just anyone at all and no one in particular" (K 31). Rather, the deconstructive "gesture is performed by the one who signs [. . .] in his own manner, [. . .] according to some idiom" (K 31). In fact, Kamuf argues that because each "deconstructive gesture" is not neutral and is always enacted by someone in particular, its force arises from an accompanying affirmation that would have "the nature of love" (K 29). Yet this someone in particular, who declares her love in order to sign in her own manner, in her own idiom, and thus in her own name, does not exist "outside or before the passion of the subject's address of love" (K 31). Kamuf writes: "Determined by the other, the address of love is never issued by a pre-existing subject in the direction of an object, its object, or destination" (K 30). Rather, the self of which Kamuf speaks is a "subject of declaration" who, in declaring her love by appropriating, hence ex-appropriating, the other's address, would sign in her own name. And, she, as Derrida says of Echo, would sign "her own love" (DM).

Counter-Signature

The tables have now turned. The words that return to Narcissus, the sounds that reach his ears, are no longer his own. For Echo's "voice" has rendered his words foreign and unrecognizable, and Narcissus receives them as from an other. It is he, Narcissus, who now hearkens to Echo's call *to come*, who takes up and takes in her words, and who is destined to echo her. In this strange turn of events, Derrida's Narcissus seems to be subject to the same sovereign injunction that binds Echo. Narcissus, Derrida recounts, "manages to catch the end of a sentence that she sends back and makes another sentence with it" (POR 15). In replying, in resending the sentence that she has sent to him, Narcissus counter-signs Echo's signature, "making it that it is she who speaks and these are her words" (POR 15); for, "it is the ear of the other that signs"; that is to say, the other counter-signs (EO 51).

In conclusion, we recall that there can be no signature without a counter-signature, no call without a counter-call, no self without the other. Hence, for Echo's story to be heard, for the lessons she teaches about another *narcissism* to be learned, one must have ears to hear her. As Derrida says in *The Ear of the Other*, it is only "[w]hen, much later, the other will have perceived with a keen-enough ear what I will have addressed or destined to him or her, then my signature will have taken place" (EO 51). It is Derrida who has ears to hear Echo again and anew; that is, to hear her otherwise, because, like Echo, he knows that in order "[t]o hear and understand [. . .], one must also produce" (EO 51). Thus, Derrida writes in *Rogues* that "Echo thus lets be heard (*laisse alors entendre*) by whoever wants to hear it, by whoever might love hearing it, something other than what she seems to be saying" (R xii/10). In this allegory of Echo, one hears, if one listens well, another narrative of narcissism, which does not disavow mourning and opens itself to the experience of the other *as* other.

Afterword. Narcissism—By What Right?

A claim one would be right to consider exorbitant, especially if it comes together in a single person or in the unity of a homogeneous discourse. That
this is not the case and that this very hypothesis is structurally untenable already complicates the very idea of such a claim, but not without also and at
the same time compromising the identity, unity, and assembling of an insti-
tution founded upon such a project. But is it not the example of the untenable
hypothesis, the impossible project, that we are invoking?

—Jacques Derrida, *Who's Afraid of Philosophy? Right to Philosophy* I

After sketching out new configurations of narcissism, which
have so little in common with the numerous figures and forms
of autonomy that the West has generated, one might still want
to ask "By what *right?*" That is to say, by what right [*droit*] or
according to what law [*droit*] could one be justified in one's
narcissism? If, as Derrida so persuasively argues in *Rogues* and
elsewhere, the Western notion of rights—first and foremost
the right to regard oneself as a man—has been fundamentally
bound up with the phantasm of the sovereign self and is predicated on the supposed autonomy of the *ipse*, then an appeal
to a "right" to a deconstructed notion of narcissism seems to be
an absurd one. Indeed, as we showed in the Introduction,
"rights claims" in the name of the proper (self, clan, nation,
property, etc.) are inseparable from the classical conception of

narcissism as the desire for the One. Throughout his writing, Derrida seems to suggest that all appeals to the proper establishment of rights runs the risk of, if not aims at, setting up the proper of man.

Then, let us ask again "By what *right?*" By what right is an *im-possible* narcissism—a narcissism predicated on the other and thus is in advance without mastery—legitimated? Our answer must be by no proper right, or rather by no right to the proper. Thus, by way of conclusion, we would like to suggest that one ought not hear Derrida's call for the rehabilitation of the "right to narcissism" (*le droit au narcissisme*) as an appeal to some natural law or some new juridical or political claim (although a politics and jurisprudence to-come would need to reckon with this new "ethics" of narcissism). If, in the light of our analyses of Rousseau, Kristeva, and Derrida, the notion of narcissism has undergone a significant transformation, even a metamorphosis, then the *right* in the invocation to a "right to narcissism" must also be thought anew. Such a reexamination of the Western notion of right, which is inseparable from our philosophical and political conceptions of the self, is beyond the scope of this book. We can only gesture toward another "right" that would, like our reconfigured "narcissism(s)," be based on a new understanding of self-relation in which to speak of and for oneself would, as Echo knew well, pass by way of and be indebted to the other. This "right" to come, which is yet to be invented, would require both a work of mourning for the loss of the phantasmatic potency of the "I can" ("*je peux*") and a new affirmation of and passion for an ex-appropriating "self," that is, an im-possible narcissism.

Notes

1. Jacques Derrida with Marie-Françoise Plissart, *Right of Inspection*, trans. David Wills (New York: Monacelli Press, 1998); *Droit de regard* (Paris: Minuit, 1985) (hereafter cited in text as RI).

2. Although terms for self-love exist in numerous Indo-European languages and some predate the Ovidian myth of Narcissus, the word "narcissism" is a fairly recent linguistic invention. Freud inherits this term and modern psychological concept from two contemporaries, Havelock Ellis and Paul Näcke. In 1898, the British Ellis described a psychological attitude in which an individual treats his own body as a sexual object, calling this behavior "narcissus-like." A year later, in his *Die sexuellen Perversitäten*, Näcke further describes this perverse attitude and gives this disorder a name—"*Narzissismus.*" Freud appropriates both the term and the concept and attempts to integrate these accounts into psychoanalysis. In his earliest treatment of narcissism in his 1910 study of Leonardo da Vinci, Freud uses the term to designate and explain the type of object choice in homosexual males, hence varying little from the meaning Ellis and Näcke gave to narcissism in their writings. However, in the Schreber case (1911) and in *Totem and Taboo* (1912), Freud describes narcissism as a stage

in psychosexual development between autoeroticism and object love, in which the eroticization at work is not directed toward one's body but is invested in one's thoughts, overvaluing their powers and attributing to them a magical omnipotence. In his well-known 1914 piece "On Narcissism: An Introduction," Freud extends and complicates his notion of narcissism further, integrating it into psychoanalytic theory more broadly. Narcissism appears not as a mere perversion (although certain forms of "secondary narcissism" are indeed pathological for Freud), but emerges as a normal and universal structure in which the ego as such is invested with libido. Further, the ego is now portrayed as a reservoir of libido that flows in and out, and thus is the source of both love of the self and love of the other. Freud's account of narcissism, and its various forms, is hardly uniform across his corpus. As readers of his work know, it is a highly complex and mobile concept. For a concise and insightful analysis of narcissism in Freud, see Chapter 4, "The Ego and Narcissism," in Jean Laplanche, *Life and Death in Psychoanalysis*, trans. Jeffrey Mehlman, (Baltimore: Johns Hopkins University Press, 1976); *Vie et mort en psychanalyse*, (Paris: Flammarion, 1970).

In their uptake of this notion, practitioners of modern psychology and psychiatry have reduced narcissism to a set of pathological attitudes and behaviors, which has yielded our commonplace understanding of the term as "egoism" or "megalomania." This conception of narcissism as egoism has become predominant in contemporary analyses of culture, most famously in Christopher Lasch's *The Culture of Narcissism: American Life in an Age of Diminishing Expectations* (New York: Norton, 1979).

3. Jacques Derrida, *H. C. for Life, That Is to Say . . .*, trans. Laurent Milesi and Stefan Herbrechter (Palo Alto, Calif.: Stanford University Press, 2006), 115; *H. C. pour la vie, c'est a dire . . .* (Paris; Galilée, 2002), 115 (hereafter cited in text as HC).

4. Jean-Jacques Rousseau, *The First and Second Discourses and Essay on the Origin of Languages,* ed., trans., and annotated Victor Gourevitch (New York: Harper & Row, 1986), 149–50; *Oeuvres complètes*, vol. III, ed. Bernard Gagnebin, Marcel Raymond, et al. (Paris: NRF-Editions de la Pléiade, 1959–1995), 143 (hereafter cited in text as SD/OC III).

5. We will follow Rousseau's usage of the term "man" (*l'homme*) to distinguish the human animal from the beast. For the justification for this decision, see note 6 in Part I, "Rousseau: The Passions of Narcissus."

6. As we will see in more detail in Chapter 1, "Man's Double Birth," savage man's heart was alone and his own existence was his sole preoccupation.

7. Note Rousseau's use of "*considérer*," which weaves together the older usage indicating "to esteem, respect, and revere" with the more commonplace sense of looking attentively.

8. Julia Kristeva, *Nations without Nationalism* (New York: Columbia University Press, 1993) (hereafter cited in text as NWN).

9. Sigmund Freud, *Group Psychology and the Analysis of the Ego*, trans. James Strachey, in *The Standard Edition of the Complete Psychological Works of Sigmund Freud*, vol. 18 (London: Hogarth Press, 1966), 102 (hereafter cited in text as SE 18).

10. In one of her earliest works, Kristeva suggests that an "ethics" (concerning textual practices and meanings) would require a "negativizing of narcissism." See *Revolution in Poetic Language*, trans. Margaret Waller (New York: Columbia University Press, 1984), 233; *La révolution du language poétique* (Paris: Editions du Seuil, 1974), 203. By "negativizing" narcissism, Kristeva does not mean a simple negation of narcissism as such, in favor of something like nonnarcissism. Rather, if "narcissism," in this early and more conventional usage of the term in Kristeva's corpus, indicates the seeming "unity of the subject" and certain fixations associated with it, then the "negativizing of narcissism" would entail the disclosing of the heterogeneity at play in the formation of the subject and its truths. This "ethical function," according to Kristeva, can be fulfilled only insofar as "it pluralizes, pulverizes, 'musicates' these truths" (233). In Part II, "Kristeva: The Rebirth of Narcissus," we will show that, in her later analyses of narcissism and love, Kristeva has applied this "ethical" mode of interpretation to the notion of narcissism itself, offering an "ethical" account of this "experience" or, as we will see, the structure of subjectivity, which is shown to be rich, complex, and heterogeneous. Kristeva's reworked notion of narcissism and its structures, especially as it is developed in *Tales of Love*, reveals an open and malleable system rather than a closed and rigid one.

For an insightful analysis of the "negativization of narcissism" and the ethical relationship with the wholly other, in which Ewa Plonowska Ziarek brings Kristeva in conversation with Levinas, see Ziarek's "The Libidinal Economy of Power, Democracy, and the Ethics of Psychoanalysis" in *An Ethics of Dissensus: Postmodernity, Feminism, and the Politics of Radical Democracy* (Palo Alto, Calif.: Stanford University Press, 2001).

11. We will not need to look further than this text to see Kristeva reworking the notion of narcissism—juxtaposing an "oceanic" or objectless narcissism, which is lethal for both self and other, with a narcissistic structure that will open up the possibility of an "an optimal narcissistic image" that will not be reactive or defensive (NWN 52). Kristeva goes as far as to suggest that a healthy group identity is not only possible but also necessary: "National pride is comparable, from a psychological standpoint, to the *good narcissistic image* that the child gets from its mother and proceeds, through the intersecting play of identification demands emanating from both parents, to elaborate an ego ideal. By not being aware of, underestimating, or degrading such a narcissistic image or ego ideal, one humiliates and lays subject or group open to *depression*" (52). One should add that, for Kristeva, it is clear that this dangerous naïveté regarding narcissism runs the risk not simply of depression but also of more extreme forms of violence toward self and other.

12. In the chapter entitled *"Comme si, comme ça*: Following Derrida on the Phantasms of the Self, the State, and a Sovereign God," in *Derrida from Now On* (New York: Fordham University Press, 2008), Michael Naas argues for the "special use and status" of the term "phantasm" in Derrida's work (189). He provides a comprehensive and thoughtful survey of the appearances of this term throughout Derrida's corpus, from *Voice and Phenomenon* to *Glas*, from "Faith and Knowledge" to "Auto-immunity: Real and Symbolic Suicides." Naas notes that Derrida uses *fantasme* interchangeably with *phantasme* in his writings and cites Derrida from *Paper Machine*, where he writes that phantasm "condenses all together image, spectrality, and simulacrum—and the weight of desire, the libidinal investment of affect" (*Paper Machine* 63, cited in Naas 194).

If Derrida's work, from the very beginning, put into question any putatively pure origin, pure autoaffection, pure presence, and any indivisible, inviolable center, the phantasm, Naas claims, is what leads us to believe in the coincidence of the self with itself, in immediate self-apprehension. The phantasm thus is "nothing other than our belief in a phenomenon that transcends itself, that spontaneously gives rise to itself" (192). The phantasm, it is important to underscore, would be "what our desire cannot fail to be tempted into believing" (*Speech and Phenomenon* 104, in Naas, 192). What gives the phantasm its enduring influence, persistence, and effectiveness, he emphasizes, is not its ontological status, but its staying or returning power, "its *regenerative* power" (192). "Deconstruction would thus be," Naas's chapter expertly shows, "first and foremost, a deconstruction of the phantasm" (191). For "the phantasm needs to be exposed and denounced not because it is untrue, false, or merely apparent but because it is so powerful it threatens the very freedom that makes it possible" (197). If "every form of sovereignty thus appears to be a phantasm, and every phantasm a phantasm of sovereignty," then a certain narcissism, as the desire for pure autonomy and absolute self-coincidence, is nothing other than a phantasm of sovereignty that must be perpetually deconstructed (195). This will be the spirit in which we will be employing the term "phantasm" throughout.

13. Jacques Derrida, *Rogues: Two Essays on Reason,* trans. Pascale-Anne Brault and Michael Naas (Palo Alto, Calif.: Stanford University Press, 2005), 12; *Voyous: deux essays sur la raison* (Paris: Galilée, 2003) (hereafter cited in text as R).

14. André Green, *Life Narcissism, Death Narcissism*, trans. Andrew Weller (London: Free Association Press, 2001), 25; *Narcissisme de vie, narcissisme de mort* (Paris: Les Éditions de Minuit, 1983), 55.

15. Jacques Derrida, *Specters of Marx: The State of the Debt, the Work of Mourning, and the New International,* trans. Peggy Kamuf (New York: Routledge, 1994), 98; *Spectres de Marx: l'état de la dette, le travail du deuil et la nouvelle internationale* (Paris: Galilée, 1993), 161–62 (hereafter cited in text as SM).

16. We have very gently modified David Wills's excellent translation here.

17. For detailed chapter overviews, see the introductions to Parts I, II, and III: "Another Morality Tale?," "Self-Love—Beyond Sin, Symptoms, and Sublime Values," and "The Very Concept of Narcissism," respectively.

18. Jacques Derrida, "A Certain Impossible Possibility of Saying the Event" in *Critical Inquiry* 33 (2007): 454; "Une certaine possibilité impossible de dire l'événement" in *Dire l'événement, est-ce possible? Seminaire de Montreal, pour Jacques Derrida* (Paris: L'Harmattan, 2001), 100. For Derrida's discussion of the notion of the impossible, see "Deconstructions: The Im-possible," Michael Taormina in *French Theory in America,* ed. Sylvère Lotringer and Sande Cohen (New York: Routledge, 2001), 18, 21–25, 26, 28, 30 and *Aporias,* trans. Thomas Dutoit (Palo Alto, Calif.: Stanford University Press, 1993; *Apories* (Paris: Galilée, 1996).

PART I. ROUSSEAU: THE PASSIONS OF NARCISSUS

1. For the use of *amour-propre* in the writings of the French moralists of the seventeenth century, including L'abbé de Saint-Cyran (1581–1643), Madame de Sablé (1599–1678), La Rochefoucauld (1613–80), Damien Mitton (1618–90), Pascal (1623–62), and Noël d'Argonne (1634–1704), see Jean Lafond, ed., *Moralistes du XVIIe Siècle* (Paris: Robert Laffont, 1992).

2. See Augustine's *City of God.*

3. Voltaire, *Le Siècle de Louis XIV* in *Oeuvres historiques,* ed. René Pomeau (Paris: Gallimard, 1957), Pléiade edition, 1004. Also, see La Rochefoucauld, *Maximes,* ed. Jacques Truchet (Paris: Garnier-Flammarion, 1977).

4. Jean-Jacques Rousseau, "Narcissus; or, the Lover of Himself" in *Letter to D'Alembert and Writings for the Theater. The Collected Writings of Rousseau,* vol. 10, ed. and trans. Allan Bloom, Charles Butterworth, and Christopher Kelly (Hanover, N.H.: University Press of New England, 2004); *Narcisse ou l'amant de lui-même* in *Oeuvres complètes,* vol. II, ed. Bernard Gagnebin, Marcel Raymond, et al. (Paris: NRF-Editions de la Pléiade, 1959–95).

Of all the pieces of theatrical literature that he penned, *Narcissus* seems to have played an important role in Rousseau's life over several decades. Around the age of twenty (circa 1732), he wrote the first version of the drama, which he carried in his bag with him when he headed to Paris in 1742 in the hope of finding success in writing for the stage. Over the next decade, he reworked the play with the assistance of Marivaux, France's most renowned playwright of the eighteenth century. *Narcissus* is finally performed in Paris in December 1752 by the Comédie Française. The play's poor reception and early closing was a great disappointment to the forty-year-old Rousseau, who a year later in a text entitled "Preface to *Narcissus*" abandons this play, along with his other theatrical works, like a bastard child. "They are illegitimate children one still fondles with pleasure while blushing to be their father, of whom takes one's final leave, and whom one sends off to seek their fortune without greatly worrying about what will become of them." See Jean-Jacques Rousseau, "Preface to *Narcissus*" in *The First and Second Discourses and Essay on the Origin of Languages,* ed., trans., and annotated Victor Gourevitch (New York: Harper & Row, 1986), 99–100; "Préface de *Narcisse*" in *Oeuvres complètes,* vol. II, ed. Bernard Gagnebin, Marcel Raymond, et al. (Paris: NRF-Editions de la Pléiade, 1959–95), 963 (hereafter cited in text as PN/OC II).

5. Paul de Man, *Allegories of Reading: Figural Language in Rousseau, Nietzsche, Rilke, and Proust* (New Haven, Conn.: Yale University Press, 1979), 165 (hereafter cited in text as AR). For a complex and persuasive interpretation of *Narcissus* as well as Rousseau's play *Pygmalion,* see Chapter 8, "Self (Pygmalion)," of the same text. For another compelling, albeit quite different, analysis of Rousseau's *Narcissus,* see Louis Marin, "Entreglose 1. L'image travestie" in *Des pouvoirs de l'image: gloses* (Paris: Seuil, 1993). In his fascinating reading of the play, Marin not only addresses questions of autoaffection and biography but also explores sexual ambiguity and anxiety.

6. We will follow throughout Rousseau's usage of the term man (*l'homme*) to distinguish the human animal from the beast. We will do so, in part, to remain close to the language of his texts and, in part, to allow the sexual position of the "savage" (*Second Discourse*) and the "child" (*Emile*) not to be obscured by importing gender-neutral terminology.

7. In the *Second Discourse,* Rousseau attempts to wrest the passions from the lowly place they have been accorded by the moralists: "Regardless of what the Moralists may say about it, human understanding owes much to the Passions which, as is commonly admitted, also owe much to it: It is by their activity that our reason perfects itself; we seek to know only because we desire to enjoy, and it is not possible to conceive of why someone without desires or fears would

take the trouble of reasoning. The Passions, in turn, owe their origins to our needs, and their progress to our knowledge; for one can desire or fear things only in terms of one's ideas about them, or by the simple impulsion of Nature." Jean-Jacques Rousseau, *The First and Second Discourses and Essay on the Origin of Languages,* ed., trans., and annotated Victor Gourevitch (New York: Harper & Row, 1986), 149–50; *Oeuvres complètes,* vol. III, ed.Bernard Gagnebin, Marcel Raymond, et al. (Paris: NRF-Editions de la Pléiade, 1959–95), 143.

8. As the meaning of and relationship between these two terms—*amour de soi* and *amour-propre*—are at issue in the entirety of Part I, we have chosen to leave these expressions untranslated throughout. *Amour de soi* has been commonly rendered as "love of self" or been left in the French, while *amour-propre* has routinely been rendered as "vanity." As our entire argument in this part relies upon taking another, indeed a closer, look at how these terms function within Rousseau's corpus, it is necessary to suspend the task of translation.

9. For Rousseau, although the "source of all the passions is sensibility," the "imagination determines their bent" (E 219/OC IV:501). Therefore, man's imagination can direct the passions for good or ill, and "the errors of imagination" are responsible for "transform[ing] into vices the passions of all limited beings" (E 219/OC IV:501).

10. Jean-Jacques Rousseau, *Emile or On Education,* introduced, trans., with notes by Allan Bloom (New York: Basic Books, 1979), 212–13; *Oeuvres complètes,* vol. IV, ed. Bernard Gagnebin, Marcel Raymond, et al. (Paris: NRF-Editions de la Pléiade, 1959–95), 491 (hereafter cited in text as E/OC IV).

I. MAN'S DOUBLE BIRTH

1. In Book IV of *Emile,* Rousseau describes the two forms of education that are appropriate for the two epochs of man's existence: "The study suitable for man is that of his relations. So long as he knows himself only in his physical being, he ought to study himself in his relations with things. This is the job of childhood. When he begins to sense his moral being, he ought to study himself in his relations with men. This is the job of his whole life" (E 214/OC IV:493).

2. "Emile," Rousseau writes, "has only natural and purely physical knowledge. He does not know even the name of history, or what metaphysics or morals are" (E 207/OC IV:487).

3. In the *Second Discourse*, Rousseau strongly argues that although man in his natural condition may be ignorant of distinctions between right and wrong he ought not be thought of as immoral. In particular, he challenges Hobbes's portrait of savage man as innately evil: "Above all, let us not conclude with Hobbes that because he has no idea of goodness, man is naturally wicked, that he is vicious because he does not know virtue, that he always refuses to those of his kind services which he does not believe he owes them, or that by virtue of the right which he with reason assigns himself to the things he needs, *he insanely imagines himself to be the sole owner of the entire Universe*" (SD159/OC III:153, emphasis mine). Rousseau attributes this misunderstanding of man in the state of nature to the projection of social man's (im)moral character onto the savage. For when certain philosophers were "continually speaking of need, greed, oppression, desires, and pride transferred to the state Nature ideas they had taken from society," Rousseau asserts, "they spoke of Savage Man and depicted Civil man" (SD 139/OC III:132). For Rousseau, this narcissistic delusion of Hobbes's natural man is, in fact, a retroactive and fictive projection by civil man, who is deluded by a pathological *amour propre*.

4. NJH Dent, in his *A Rousseau Dictionary* (Cambridge, Mass.: Blackwell, 1992), describes Rousseau's idiosyncratic use of the term "moral" as "the assumption of 'moral being'—that is, coming to understand oneself and other people, and one's relationships in terms of titles, obligations, and responsibilities and so on—is for Rousseau a crucial element in human development" (163).

5. Therefore, Rousseau can argue that *amour de soi*, as it is in accordance with nature, is "always good and always in conformity with order" (E 213/OC IV:491).

6. In the *Second Discourse*, Rousseau writes that as the savage's "mind could not frame abstract ideas of regularity and of proportion, so his heart cannot feel the sentiments of admiration and love that arise, without our even noticing it, from applying these ideas; he heeds only the temperament he received from Nature, and not a taste which he could not have acquired, and *any woman suits him*" (SD 164/OC 3:158, emphasis mine).

7. For a detailed analysis of this movement outside one's being, see Lawrence Cooper, "Between Eros and Will to Power: Rousseau and 'The Desire to Extend Our Being,'" *The American Political Science Review* 98, no. 1 (Feb. 2004): 105–19.

8. When we employ the word "vanity" in this chapter, we are exclusively referring to Rousseau's use of the term "*la vanité*" and not to *amour-propre*, which can in some, but certainly not all, contexts mean vanity.

9. Jacques Derrida, *Of Grammatology,* trans. Gayatry Chakravorty Spivak (Baltimore: Johns Hopkins University Press, 1976), 178; *De la grammatologie* (Paris: Minuit, 1967) (hereafter cited in text as OG).

10. It is interesting to note that Rousseau contends that moral love and the nefarious passions it stirs up are not simply "born of social practice" as such but are manipulated "with much skill and care by women in order to establish their rule and to make dominant the sex which should obey" (SD 164/OC III:158).

11. For example, see Pauline Chazan's "Rousseau as Psycho-Social Moralist: The Distinction between *Amour de soi* and *Amour-propre*" in *History of Philosophy Quarterly* 10, no. 4 (October 1993): 341–54. Against more positive interpretations of the place of *amour-propre* in Rousseau's work, in particular NJH Dent's *Rousseau* (New York: Basil Blackwell, 1989), Chazan claims that "for Rousseau amour-propre has no rightful place whatever in our lives" (347), and "if *amour-propre* is a technical term that names a disorder, it can have no place at all in man's living with others" (348).

2. REGARDING SELF-LOVE ANEW

1. NJH Dent, "Rousseau on *Amour-propre,*" *Proceedings of the Aristotelian Society* 71, 2 (1998): 56–73, 67. In addition to Dent's important reinterpretation of the notion of *amour-propre* and its relationship to *amour de soi,* there are other nuanced readings of these two forms of self-love in Rousseau's writings. For example, see M. E. Brint, "Echoes of Narcissus," *Political Theory* 16, no. 4 (Nov. 1988): 617–35; Juliet Flower MacCannell, "Nature and Self-love: A Reinterpretation of Rousseau's 'Primitive Passion,'" *PMLA* 92, no. 5 (Oct. 1977): 890–902; Timothy O'Hagan, "Rousseau on *Amour-Propre:*

On Six Facets of *Amour-Propre*," *Proceedings of the Aristotelian Society* 99, no. 1 (1999): 91–108.

2. In Chapter 7, "Metaphor (*Second Discourse*)," of *Allegories of Reading*, de Man offers a more sympathetic reading of the *Discourse on Inequality* than we are providing here.

3. Jacques Derrida, "Passions: 'An Oblique Offering,'" trans. David Wood in *Derrida: A Critical Reader*, ed. David Wood (Cambridge, Mass.: Blackwell, 1992), 12; *Passions* (Paris: Galilée, 1993), 33. We will return to this text in the introduction, "The Very Concept of Narcissism," to Part III.

4. Rousseau claims that animals also show signs of *pitié*—"one daily sees the repugnance of Horses to trample a living Body underfoot; an animal never goes past a dead animal of its own Species without some restlessness" (SD 160/OC III:154).

5. *Pitié*, in Rousseau's account, is not only the first and only natural virtue (which takes the place of morals and laws in the State of Nature), but also it gives rise to all other social virtues. He writes "from this single attribute flow all the social virtues [. . .]. Indeed, what are generosity, Clemency, Humanity, if not Pity applied to the weak, the guilty, or the species in general? Even Benevolence and friendship, properly understood, are the products of a steady pity focused on a particular object" (SD 161–62/OC III:155).

6. An important clause, which we have underscored, was omitted in the Bloom translation of the following passage: "pour adoucir [. . .] la férocité de son amour propre, *ou avant la naissance de cet amour*, tempere l'ardeur qu'il a pour son bien être." I have included a translation of this clause in the citation above.

7. Jean-Jacques Rousseau, *Essay on the Origin of Languages*, ed. and trans. Victor Gourevitch (New York: Harper & Row, 1986), 261; *Oeuvres complètes*. vol. 5, ed. Bernard Gagnebin, Marcel Raymond, et al. (Paris: NRF-Editions de la Pléiade, 1959–1995), 395 (hereafter cited in text as EOL/OC V).

8. For an interesting analysis of the notion of "identification" and its relation to self-love in Rousseau, see Pierre Force's "Self-love, Identification, and the Origin of Political Economy" in *Yale French Studies*, no. 92, *Exploring the Conversable World*, ed. Elena Russo (1997): 46–64.

9. Rousseau argues that prior to the full functioning of the imagination that the child "not imagining what others feel, knows only his own ills" and thus exhibits a lack of empathy (E 222/OC IV:504). Rousseau also contends that an individual in the throes of suffering is unable to imagine the woes of another and thus cannot be moved by *pitié*: "When one has suffered or fears suffering, one pities those who suffer; but when one is suffering, one pities only oneself [*Quand on a souffert, ou qu'on craint de souffrir, on plaint ceux qui souffrent; mais tandis qu'on souffre, on ne plain que soi*]" (E 229/OC IV:514). Both the child and the individual in pain are closed off from others as others and feel only the weight of their own existences. It is interesting to note that in his seminal essay "On Narcissism," Freud also employs the examples of the child's self-satisfaction and the sick person's self-absorption to illustrate the narcissistic disposition.

10. The child's capacity for imagination will awaken over time as will his fear of death. The child, "having reflected little on sensitive beings, will know late what it is to suffer and die. He will begin to have gut reactions at the sounds of complaints and cries, the sight of blood flowing will make him avert his eyes; the convulsions of a dying animal will cause him an ineffable distress before he knows whence come these new movements within him" (E 222/OC IV:505). A few pages later, Rousseau adds: "It is noted in general that all men are affected sooner and more generally by wounds, cries, groans, the apparatus of painful operations, and all that brings objects of suffering to the sense. The idea of destruction, since it is more complex, is not similarly striking; the image of death has a later and weaker effect because no one has within himself the experience of death. One must have seen corpses to feel the agonies of the dying. But when this image has been well formed in our mind, there is no spectacle more horrible to our eyes" (E 226/OC IV:511).

11. On Derrida's reading, "the animal does have a potential faculty of *pitié*, but it imagines neither the suffering of the other *as such* nor the passage from suffering to *death*" (OG 187/265).

12. If we find our common identity in our sufferings, then, as Rousseau declares in the "First Maxim" of *pitié*, it "is not in the human heart to put ourselves in the place of people who are happier than we, but only in that of those who are more pitiable" (E 223/OC IV:506).

13. We have gently modified the Bloom translation here.

14. Rousseau contends that by taking the youth out of himself through the experience of *pitié* one will "excite in him goodness, humanity, commiseration, beneficence, and all the attractive and sweet passions naturally pleasing to men" rather than "envy, covetousness, hate, and all the repulsive and cruel passions which make sensibility, so to speak, not only nothing but negative and torment the man who experiences them" (E 223/OC IV:506).

15. "[I]t must be remembered," Rousseau reveals, "that all these means by which I take my pupil out of himself, always have, nevertheless, a direct relation to him; for not only does he get inner enjoyment from them, but also, in making him beneficent for the profit of others" (E 253/OC IV:548).

16. In his take on the "economy of *pitié*," Derrida argues that for Rousseau the movement of identification ought not be complete, as self-protection is paramount. In his gloss on Rousseau's position, Derrida writes: "We neither can nor should feel the pain of others [*autrui*] immediately and absolutely, for such an interiorization or identification would be dangerous and destructive. That is why the imagination, the reflection, and the judgment that arouse *pitié* also limit its power and hold the suffering of the other at a certain distance. One knows this suffering for what it is, one pities others, but one protects oneself [. . .]. The paradox of the relation to the other is clearly articulated [. . .] the more you identify with the other [*s'identifie à l'autre*], the better you feel his suffering as *his* [*la sienne*]: our own suffering is that of the other [*l'autre*]. That of the other [*l'autre*], as itself, must remain the other's. There is no authentic identification except in a certain nonidentification, etc." (OG 190/269). Thus, in his interpretation of these passages on identification and nonidentification, Derrida suggests that Rousseau only "permits" the self to be exposed to the other in order to better distance itself and thus inoculate itself from the other.

PART II. KRISTEVA: THE BIRTH OF NARCISSUS

1. Julia Kristeva, *L'amour de soi et ses avatars. Démesure et limites de la sublimation* (Nantes: Editions Pleins Feux, 2005), 7. (hereafter cited in text as AS). All translations of this text are my own.

2. For their discussions of *philautia*, see Book IX of Aristotle's *Nichomachean Ethics* and the following sections—"Duties to One-self," "Proper Self-Respect," and "Self-Love"—of Kant's *Lectures on Ethics*. For Plotinus and Aquinas's treatments of self-love, see respectively the Sixth Tractate of the First Book of the *Enneads* and the Third Book of the *Commentary on Sentences*. In addition to Rousseau (whose notions of *amour de soi* and *amour-propre* were addressed fully in Part I of the book), a number of French moralists from the seventeenth and eighteenth centuries prominently thematized "self-love" in their writings. In particular, see La Rochefoucauld's *Maxims*, La Fontaine's *Fables*, and Pascal's *Pensées*.

3. Julia Kristeva, *Hannah Arendt*, trans. Ross Guberman (New York: Columbia University Press, 2001), *Le génie féminin*: Tome I *Hannah Arendt* (Paris: Fayard, 1999); *Melanie Klein*, trans. Ross Guberman (New York: Columbia University Press, 2004) (hereafter cited in text as MK), Tome II *Melanie Klein* (Paris: Fayard, 2000); *Colette*, trans. Jane Marie Todd (New York: Columbia University Press, 2004), Tome III *Colette* (Paris: Fayard, 2002).

4. Julia Kristeva, *Tales of Love*, trans. Leon Roudiez (New York: Columbia University Press, 1987); *Histoires d'amour* (Paris: Editions Denoël, 1983) (hereafter cited in text as TL).

5. I have slightly modified Roudiez's translation here to allow the reader to better hear Kristeva's emphasis on *singularity*, which, although long stressed in her work as a resistance to totalitarian tendencies, has been highlighted in her recent writings on feminine genius. In order to fully justify this emphasis, it would be necessary to trace Kriteva's uses of the adjective *singulier* and noun *la singularitié* in these texts and map their relationship to sexual identity.

6. With the marriage of Neoplatonism and Christian dogma, a new incarnation of Narcissus is sketched out in the writings of Augustine and Aquinas. Kristeva writes that Narcissus "is compensated for by the genius of speculative thought, starting with Plotinus and up to the Fathers of the Church who rehabilitate the narcissian concern for one's own proper space, beyond the condemnation of the narcissistic error" (TL 376/467). See "God Is Love" and "Ratio Diligendi, or the Triumph of One's Own. Thomas Aquinas: Natural Love and Love of Self" in Part IV, as well as "Extraterrestrials Suffering for Want of Love" in Part VI, of *Tales of Love*.

7. If God is defined as love, specifically as *agape* (a disinterested gift that is bestowed upon the believer regardless of his worthiness to receive it), then it is with this love that the believer identifies and gives rise to a "mixture of affect, desire, and meaning" that permits the child of God to love himself, as Augustine writes in *The City of God*, "for and because of God" (TL 171/218). This identification with God, via "the agape of the Cross" (TL 377/468), "promises salvation to narcissism" (TL 378/469). According to Kristeva, what makes the Christian religion capable of conferring salvation is that "it creates a space for love that takes into account the illusion, the seeming, and the impossible settled at the very heart of supreme reality—at the heart of the relationship with the Loved One [. . .] which is defined only through belonging to the One" (TL 123/155).

8. It is essential to point out that at times in her writing Kristeva will also employ the word "narcissism" to refer to a symptom or set of symptoms. For example, in *New Maladies of the Soul,* trans. Ross Guberman (New York: Columbia University Press, 1995) (hereafter cited in text as NMS); *Les nouvelles maladies de l'âme* (Paris: Fayard, 1993), she discusses the conditions under which the "'I' run[s] the risk of falling into the indifference of a narcissistic, lethal fusion" (119). This usage of the adjective "narcissistic" is not uncommon in Kristeva's texts when she is outlining the features of a pathological "narcissistic personality." However, our reading does not focus on psychoanalytic disorders that are labeled "narcissistic," because we would like to suggest that the emergence of what analysts describe as a "narcissistic symptom" is ultimately a failure of narcissism or, as Kristeva would describe it, the failure to adequately elaborate the "narcissistic structure."

9. Sara Beardsworth, *Julia Kristeva: Psychoanalysis and Modernity* (Albany: State University of New York Press, 2004), 57 (hereafter cited in text as SB).

10. For some other accounts of narcissism in Kristeva's works, see, for example, Sara Beardsworth, "Freud's Oedipus and Kristeva's Narcissus: Three Heterogeneities," *Hypatia* 20, no. 1 (Winter 2005): 54–77; Cynthia Chase, "Primary Narcissism and the Giving of Figure: Kristeva with Hertz and de Man," in *Abjection, Melancholia, and Love: The Work of Julia Kristeva,* eds. Andrew Benjamin and John Fletcher (London: Routledge, 1990); Sylvie Gambaudo, *Kristeva,*

Psychoanalysis and Culture (Hampshire: Ashgate Publishing, 2007), especially Chapters 6–8.

11. In the conclusion of *Tales of Love*, Kristeva writes: "As long as the Western Self could think of itself as an *Ego affectus est*, with Bernard of Clairvaux for instance, its psychic space—introspective space container of primary narcissism—remained safe." However, "[t]he discontent [as exemplified in our era] always arises out of a repudiation of love—of the *Ego affectus est*" (TL 378/469).

12. What Beardsworth's extensive and insightful analyses of narcissism in Kristeva's thought, which focuses almost exclusively on the "histories" of subjectivity in terms of suffering and loss, does not fully account for is Kristeva own rewriting of the notion of narcissism and her reinscription of the figure of Narcissus into this history. From our point of view, it is essential that one read Kristeva's texts on narcissism not only as descriptive or diagnostic of the "crises" of subjectivity but also as prescriptive for new narratives of "subjectivity." If one does not interpret Kristeva's Narcissus (of course, there is more than one in her texts) exclusively as a representative of a historical symptom, but rather as a malleable structure, then one ends up with a very different story and, I am convinced, a much more resourceful figure.

While, in general, I am sympathetic to Beardsworth's reading of Kristeva's portrayal of the "modern" Narcissus—"[F]or Kristeva, psychoanalysis discovers the tendential severance of the semiotic and the symbolic: the problem of modern nihilism. This is why the figure of Narcissus is apparently so ambiguous in her thought. For Narcissus shows up today in his or her infantile, regressive form, socially and symbolically abandoned. On the other hand, unacknowledged suffering is the remnant of freedom because the suffering subjectivity that Kristeva attends to—the abandoned Narcissus—is where the semiotic is lodged"—we worry that Beardsworth's interpretation, by overidentifying the narcissistic subject as a "suffering subject," neutralizes the affirmative and inventive interpretation that Kristeva provides of this (perhaps weary) figure. A figure, we believe, that Kristeva is making great efforts to rewrite and rehabilitate (SB 57).

13. Julia Kristeva, *The Portable Kristeva*, ed. Kelly Oliver (New York: Columbia University Press, 1997), 332 (hereafter cited in text as PK).

14. In the Editor's Note to the English translation of "Zur Einführung des Narzißmus," in Sigmund Freud, *The Standard Edition of the Complete Psychological Works of Sigmund Freud*, vol. 14 (London: Hogarth, 1957), Strachey provides evidence of Freud's uncertainty and dissatisfaction with his most extensive work on narcissism: "Ernst Jones tells us (1955, 340) that 'he [Freud] was very dissatisfied with the result and wrote to Abraham: 'The 'Narcissism' had a difficult labour and bears all marks of a corresponding deformation'" (14:70).

15. Julia Kristeva, *The Sense and Non-Sense of Revolt: The Powers and Limits of Psychoanalysis, Volume I*, trans. Jeanine Herman (New York: Columbia University Press, 2000), 46. *Sens et non-sens de la révolte. Pouvoirs et limites de la psychanalyse I*, (Paris: Fayard, 1996), 72 (hereafter cited in text as SNS).

16. In *L'amour de soi et ses avatars*, Kristeva claims: "It would be insufficient, even futile, to imagine that self-love is predetermined by a hypothetical biological program of conservation of the individual. We are compelled to return once again to psychoanalytic observations and theories in order to repeat that self-love is a slow, and not always possible, creation of the *speaking subject*. It is nonetheless indispensable for psychic autonomy: cornerstone of separation from the maternal container, foundation of individuation" (AS 8–9).

17. Julia Kristeva, *Powers of Horror: An Essay on Abjection*, trans. Leon S. Roudiez (New York: Columbia University Press, 1982), 13; *Pouvoirs de l'horreur: Essai sur l'abjection* (Paris: Seuil, 1980), 20 (hereafter cited in text as PH).

18. In general, I have followed Kristeva in using the masculine pronoun when referring to the child or the "narcissistic subject." I have done so for two main reasons: first, in order to avoid numerous complications in translation and citation, as I am working closely with the letter of Kristeva's texts, and second, so that I may move with some facility between referring to the figure of Narcissus and to the narcissistic subject. However, I do deviate from this practice when warranted. In particular, in the section entitled "Identifying Kristeva's Narcissus as Echo," I employ the female pronoun when showing how the narcissistic subject merges with Ovid's figure of Echo.

19. In an interview with Rosalind Coward in 1984, Kristeva commends Freud not only for his discovery of the dynamic of transference

in analysis but also for seeing the structures of transference at work in other arenas of human existence: "The word transference is a technical word, it comes from psychoanalysis. I think it was a great discovery by Freud to consider that what happens between the patient and the analyst is a sort of love which is a displacement of love-traumatism or love-disappointments from the past reality through the actual cure [. . .]. But also Freud tried to extrapolate this notion of transference from the cure itself to the whole field of human creativity: art, history, and the like" (PK 331). Yet, in *Melanie Klein*, a more recent text (2000), she seems to revise her earlier assessment and now claims that Freud's thought of transference is much more circumscribed: "Freud's invention of psychoanalysis was based on transference love, although he never completely theorized it" (MK 13). Is it not Kristeva who extends the notion of transference to the realms of love, subjectivity, and creativity?

3. RECONCEIVING FREUD'S NARCISSUS

1. Freud describes how "anaclitic" love emerges: "The first auto-erotic sexual satisfactions are experienced in connection with vital functions which serve the purpose of self-preservation. The sexual instincts are at the outset attached to the satisfaction of the ego-instincts; only later do they become independent of these, and even then we have an indication of that original attachment in the fact that the persons who are concerned with a child's feeding, care, and protection become his earliest sexual objects: that is to say, in the first instance his mother or a substitute for her [. . .] this type and source of object-choice [. . .] may be called the 'anaclitic' or 'attachment' type [*Anlehnungstypus*]" (SE 14:87).

It is necessary to provide a brief explanation on the usage of the adjective "anaclitic," which is an English neologism (that was derived from the Greek verb αναχλένω, which means "to rest upon" or "to lean on") that aims to render the German genitive "*Anlehnungs,*" often used by Freud in expressions like "*Anlehnungstypus der Objektwahl*." Obviously, translating "*Anlehnungstypus*" as "leaning-on type" or "attachment-type" rings strange in English, but "anaclitic-type" loses the everyday sense that the German substantive *die Anlehnung,* meaning "dependence" or "support," and the verb *an-*

lehnen, indicating the act of "leaning on," evokes for the German reader. See Jean Laplanche and Jean-Bertrand Pontalis, *The Language of Psychoanalysis,* trans. Donald Nicholson-Smith (New York: Norton, 1973), 29–31; *Le vocabulaire de psychanalyse,* Paris: Presses Universitaires de France, 1967.

2. Freud permits one exception to the general rule of female narcissism, and that is a woman's love for her own child, for her own flesh and blood. Of mothers, Freud writes: "In the child which they bear, a part of their own body confronts them like an extraneous object, to which, starting out from their own narcissism, they can give complete object love" (SE 14:89–90). Yet, only a paragraph later, he suggests that parental—not exclusively maternal—love is "a revival and reproduction" of primary narcissism.

3. However, it is interesting to note that in "Is There a Feminine Genius?" Kristeva seems to dispute Freud's claim that women generally love according to the narcissistic type rather than the attachment type: "[T]he link to the Other—that is, the object relation—seems to exist [for women] from early childhood and to be stronger than the narcissistic tendencies that women are traditionally said to exhibit" (498). Of the two sexes, it is, according to Kristeva, the female sex, or the feminine self, "that cannot be separated from its various attachments," whether they be "political, psychical, sensory, amorous, or literary" (499). "Is There a Feminine Genuis?" appears in *Critical Inquiry* 30 (Spring 2004): 493–504, excerpted from *Colette* (Paris: Fayard: 2002) (hereafter cited in text as FG).

4. Although the paradigmatic figure of self-love has long been male, Narcissus has always been portrayed as an ambiguous creature—neither child nor adult, neither fully boy nor girl. Thus, Narcissus, who often appears as a feminized male, is commonly depicted as an artist, a homosexual, and, at times, a woman. Although traditionally male, "vanity," or an excessive concern for one's reflection, has historically been deemed feminine and has been said to express itself most often in women. (For a fascinating study of the relation of the female self to her image in the ancient world, see Françoise Frontisi-Ducroux's contribution in the book written in conjunction with Jean-Pierre Vernant, *Dans l'œil du mirroir* [Paris: Odile Jacob, 1997]). Indeed, if woman is not the figure of Narcissus

as such, she has long been described as the purest expression of "narcissism" and all its attendant errors.

Even Simone de Beauvoir consecrates a chapter of *The Second Sex* to the narcissistic woman. See *The Second Sex,* trans. Deirdre Bair (New York: Vintage, 1989); *Le deuxième sexe* (Paris: Gallimard, 1949), t. II. In Chapter XXII, simply entitled "The Narcissist," Beauvoir echoes both the condemnation of the folly of self-love (which amounts to the absurd attempt to become God, i.e., to be the *en-soi* and the *pour-soi* at the same time) and of woman for falling prey (just like Ovid's Narcissus) to such vain deception. Beauvoir does not claim that narcissism is an essential flaw of all women, rather she argues that this weakness on the part of some women is a consequence of their frustrated attempts to take up their subjectivity: "It has sometimes been maintained that narcissism is the fundamental attitude of all women, but to extend this idea too broadly is to destroy it [. . .]. The fact is that narcissism is a well-defined process of identification, in which the ego (*le moi*) is regarded as an absolute end and the subject takes refuge from himself in it. Many other attitudes— authentic and inauthentic—are met with in woman, some of which we have already studied. But it is true that conditions lead woman more than man to turn toward herself and devote her love to herself" (629/525).

Yet, none of the aforementioned conflations between woman and "narcissism" explain Freud's uncharacteristic shift from Narcissus as male (cf. *Leonardo da Vinci and a Memory of His Childhood,* published in 1910) to female (cf. "On Narcissism: An Introduction," which appeared in 1914). As Sarah Kofman skillfully shows in *The Enigma of Woman: Woman in Freud's Writings,* trans. Catherine Porter (Ithaca: Cornell University Press, 1985); *L'énigme de la femme: La femme dans les texts de Freud* (Paris: Galilee, 1980), Freud's famous portrayal of the female sex as the sex that "lacks" is radically revised in this essay, and in this essay alone (with the exception perhaps of the figure of the virgin in "The Taboo on Virginity"). In Freud's writings both before and after the 1914 article, woman is consistently defined as a "castrated" male and is, therefore, often described as "narcissistically wounded." In fact, in "Some Psychological Consequences of the Anatomical Distinctions between the Sexes" (1925), the young girl is said to bear her lack of a penis as "a wound to her narcissism" (AD 178). Correspondingly, in all but the 1914 essay, it is the male who appears to be profoundly invested in his narcissism, that is to say, in maintaining possession of his penis, even at the cost of "losing" his first love object. Not surprisingly, Freud finds the male inclination to preserve the integrity of his genitals to be dictated by nature, as "the penis (to follow Ferenczi) owes its extraordinary high narcissistic cathexes to its organic significance for the propagation of the species" (AD 183). Therefore, Kofman is rightly suspicious of Freud's fascination with the figure of the so-called narcissistic woman, who now emerges as entirely self-sufficient and libidinally complete. This purest and truest type of woman—woman as a fantastic plenitude—arouses male envy and desire, as it is he who now lacks, since he long ago abandoned a large share of his narcissism. Thus, it seems that the narcissistic woman in Freud does not escape the phallic logic of fullness and lack, unscathed and wounded, that operates throughout his corpus. Rather, the narcissistic woman is a fetish character if there ever was one.

5. One detects more than just a hint of moral superiority that is accorded to the position of the (male) lover: "The highest plane of development of which object-libido is capable is seen in the state of being in love, when the subject seems to give up his own personality in favour of object-cathexis" (SE 14:76).

6. Sigmund Freud, *Three Essays on Theory of Sexuality*, in *The Standard Edition of the Complete Psychological Works of Sigmund Freud*, vol.7 (London: Hogarth, 1957).

7. "The breaking up of Christianity leaves these three agencies in suspense" (TL 374/464). And "the lack of a secular variant of the loving father makes contemporary discourse incapable of assuming primary identification—the substratum for our idealizing constructions" (TL 374/465). Is Kristeva's thinking of the pre-oedipal triad, which is indispensible for the formation of identity, nothing other than nostalgia for Christian subjectivity or, at least, the solid outlines that the Christian narrative has provided for the subject? For the moment, we will leave this question in abeyance and will return to it in Chapter 4, "Transference, or Amorous Dynamics."

8. The incapacity to love another has long been blamed on an excess of self-love; that is, on narcissism. Yet, it is Kristeva who shows us that the inability to love, which "leads the subject toward psychic

pain," ought not be linked to "narcissism but to autoeroticism" and hence to the failure to separate and individuate (TL 35/49).

9. See Kristeva's discussion of the temporality of birth and rebirth in the works of Arendt, Klein, and Colette, especially Colette's fascination with the metamorphoses of natality and, in particular, the "image of *hatching*" (FG 502).

10. Sigmund Freud, *The Ego and the Id*, in *The Standard Edition of the Complete Psychological Works of Sigmund Freud*, vol.19 (London: Hogarth, 1957), 31.

11. Kelly Oliver, *Reading Kristeva: Unraveling the Double-bind* (Indianapolis: Indiana University Press, 1993), 69. For other excellent analyses of Kristeva's work, see Oliver's *Family Values: Subjects between Nature and Culture* (New York: Routledge, 1997) and *Subjectivity without Subjects: From Abject Fathers to Desiring Mothers* (Lanham, Md.: Rowman & Littlefield, 1998).

12. The opposition between agape and eros—"[t]he difference between the two is that eros is a sort of ascendant movement, it tries to achieve something that is placed above, it tries to go beyond the possibilities of the person he loves; it aspires to power and is compared to an erection in the organic sense of the word. Agape is something else, it's a sort of gift, it comes to you from outside, you don't need to merit it, it's a sort of profusion"—that Kristeva employs in her work is drawn from an influential text by Nygren (PK 342). See Anders Nygren, *Agape and Eros*, trans.Philip S. Watson (Philadelphia: Westminster, 1953); *Eros et Agapè, La Notion chrétienne de l'amour et ses transformations* (Paris: Aubier, 1930, 1962).

13. Ovid, *Metamorphoses*, trans. Allen Mandelbaum (New York: Harvest, 1993), 91 (hereafter cited in text as Ovid).

14. "The subject hypercathects his own modes of expression (language, music, painting, dance, etc.) that are merged with real objects [. . .]. Thus, the child loves himself while loving—and/or while learning his mother tongue" (AS 10).

15. Although Kristeva emphasizes that the "narcissistic subject" incorporates and introjects a part-object, or simply a pattern, with which it identifies, she concurs with Freud and Klein that the child only comes to love himself through the internalization of a "good" or "loving" foreign entity. In *L'amour de soi et ses avatars* Kristeva elaborates: "Self-love constitutes itself in and through the introjec-

tion of the 'good object' (Melanie Klein has said everything on this point), and thanks to primary identification with the 'father of individual prehistory' that Freud quickly mentions in *The Ego and the Id*" (AS 9). Thus, "whatever the different varieties of identification may be, the general term 'identification' presupposes the speaking being's tendency to internalize a foreign entity, in a symbolic sense and in reality" (NMS 177/263).

16. The following passage seems to suggest that Kristeva wants the reader to recognize that infant's echoing is indeed a necessary but not a sufficient condition for primary identification to take place. "Narcissistic reiteration (when I say 'mama,' it is not yet a stable identificatory metaphor but a simple repetition) or projective identification [. . .] are elements in a series that will be completed—for the time being, never permanently—through a metaphorical movement of identification with the imaginary Father, a movement that Freud calls 'primary identification'" (NMS 179/265).

17. It should be noted that the translation of this passage does not quite capture the sense of loss that Kristeva is evoking when she portrays the musical, indeed mystical, movement of transference: "*son à l'orée de mon être, il me transfère au lieu de l'Autre à sens perdu, à perte de sens, à perte de vue.*"

18. Liddell and Scott's *Greek-English Lexicon* provides the following definitions for μεταφέρω: "To carry over, transfer"; "to change, alter"; as well as "to use a word in a changed sense, to employ a metaphor."

19. Although narcissism does not cathect a partial or whole object (like Klein's "breast"), Kristeva rejects that it is ever an objectless state. Therefore, Kristeva aligns herself with Freud's earlier articulations of narcissism as opposed to his later portrayal of "primary narcissism" as objectless, even oceanic. She clarifies her position in *Melanie Klein*: "With Freud's 'second topography' (the id, ego, and the superego), narcissism, which had been previously defined as a function of ego investment through a surge of identifications withdrawing from objects, became 'secondary narcissism.' The term 'primary narcissism,' on the other hand, was now used to describe an objectless state characterized by the total absence of any relation with other people and by a lack of any differentiation between the *ego* and the *id*. Intrauterine life and sleep are the closest approximations we

have of this objectless narcissistic state" (MK 59/96). She continues: "Indeed, if narcissism is already an internalization of an *object relation*, can we really speak of a truly objectless state? And even if an objectless state exists, which remains to be seen, the phrase 'primary narcissism' would be inapposite because it represents the beginnings of an object relation. Finally, it is difficult to understand 'just how [we are] supposed to picture the transformation from a monad shut in upon itself to a progressive discovery of the object'" (MK 59/97, emphasis mine).

20. As many of her interpreters have noted, Kristeva challenges Lacan's conception of the imaginary realm as solely specular and, by extension, the primacy of Lacan's well-known and influential theory of the "The Mirror Stage as Formative of the Function of the I as Revealed by Psychoanalytic Experience," in *Ecrits: A Selection*, trans. Alan Sheridan (New York: Norton,1977); "La stage de miroir comme formateur de la fonction du Je telle qu'elle nous est révélée dans l'expérience psychanalytique," in *Ecrits* (Paris: Seuil, 1966). In the first chapter of *Tales of Love*, Kristeva's queries about the "mirror stage"—"Does the 'mirror stage' emerge out of nowhere (*ex nihilo*)? What are the conditions of its emergence?"—imply that this stage must be conditioned by and evolve out of more archaic stages of development (TL 22/33). In *The Sense and Non-Sense of Revolt*, Kristeva reformulates the above questions to suggest that not only Lacan's "mirror stage" but also Anzieu's "skin ego," both early configurations of the self, are themselves dependent upon a triadic narcissistic structure, which includes an identification with the third. She writes: "If it is true that the skin is the first container, the archaic limit of the ego, and that the mirror is the first vector of the represented and representable identity on the other sensorial vector that is the gaze, what are the conditions for both of them occurring and becoming optimal containers? The answer is to be found in the 'father in pre-history'"; i.e., the third (SNS 54/85). See Didier Anzieu, *The Skin Ego*, trans. Chris Turner (New Haven, Conn.: Yale University Press, 1989); *Le moi-peau* (Paris: Dunod, 1985).

Further, our reading shows how Kristeva's reworking of the imaginary resists reducing "images" to the visible and expands our understanding of the imaginary as a heterogeneous domain, which is much closer to Kristeva's own description of Klein's internal, fantasized object than it is to Lacan's *imago*: "Lacan believed that narcissism takes hold through the intermediary of the object as a function of the subject's absorption into his mirror image—into the very place where he realizes that he is an Other [. . .]. And yet this spectral distortion—which, for Lacan, has the advantage of highlighting the role that the scopic function plays in structuring the ego and the object, but especially of situating the binary relationship inside the triangulation dominated by the symbolic function of the father—is bereft of the heterogeneity that characterizes Klein's notion of the internal object and of fantasy. Klein's thinking here evokes a cornucopia of images, sensations, and substances" (MK 64/104).

21. Louise Vinge, *The Narcissus Theme in Western European Literature up to the Early 19th Century* (Lund: Gleerups, 1967), 11–12.

4. TRANSFERENCE, OR AMOROUS DYNAMICS

1. Although our reading is tracing the continuity between self-love and love of the other, we should point out a fundamental difference between them. In narcissism, object relations (the distinction between subject and object, self and other) are only beginning to take shape, whereas for the lover there is an object. Even if the lover merges with the idealized Other, he nonetheless remains other. This is why Kristeva can describe the lover as "a narcissist with an *object*."

2. To emphasize the positive role that narcissism as a structure plays in making any love possible is not to forget or obscure the fact that narcissism as a symptom functions as a "barrier for love" (TL 124/156).

3. For example, see Kristeva's *In the Beginning Was Love: Psychoanalysis and Faith,* trans. Arthur Goldhammer (New York: Columbia University Press, 1987) and *This Incredible Need to Believe*, trans. Beverley Bie Brahic, (New York: Columbia University Press, 2009).

PART III. DERRIDA: THE MOURNING OF NARCISSUS

1. Jacques Derrida, *Specters of Marx: The State of the Debt, the Work of Mourning, and the New International*, trans. Peggy Kamuf (New York: Routledge, 1994), 98; *Spectres de Marx: l'état de la dette,*

le travail du deuil et la nouvelle internationale (Paris: Galilée, 1993), 161–62 (hereafter cited in text as SM).

2. To the best of my knowledge, no sustained, critical analysis of the role of narcissism or the figures of Echo and Narcissus in Derrida's thought exists. There are, however, many references made in the secondary literature to his provocative and complicated remarks about the subject.

3. Jacques Derrida, "'There Is No *One* Narcissism' (Autobiophotographies)," trans. Peggy Kamuf in *Points . . . : Interviews, 1974–1994,* selected and presented by Elisabeth Weber (Palo Alto, Calif.: Stanford University Press, 1995), 199; *Points de suspension: entretiens* (Paris: Galilée, 1992), 212 (hereafter cited in text as PS).

4. Although Freud argues that narcissism is born with the emergence of the ego as a supplement to autoeroticism, he admits that direct observation of childhood or primary narcissism is difficult, if not impossible. Hence, to find "proof" for the existence of primary narcissism, Freud directs us to view its reemergence or rebirth in the parents of a child. "If we look at the attitude of affectionate parents towards their children," Freud writes, "we have to recognize that it is a revival and reproduction of their own narcissism, which they have long since abandoned" (SE 14:90–1). Even Freud must find evidence for the existence of childhood narcissism in a parental mirror, which "ascribe[s] every perfection to the child—which sober observation would find no occasion to do" (91).

5. Jacques Derrida, *Dissemination,* trans. Barbara Johnson (Chicago: University of Chicago Press, 1981); *La Dissémination* (Paris: Seuil, 1972) (hereafter cited in text as D).

6. Jacques Derrida, "Passions: 'An Oblique Offering,'" trans. David Wood in *Derrida: A Critical Reader,* edited by David Wood (Cambridge, Mass.: Blackwell, 1992), 11–12; *Passions* (Paris: Galilée, 1993), 31–32 (hereafter cited in text as PAS).

7. In Pascale-Anne Brault and Michael Naas's editors' introduction, "To Reckon with the Dead: Jacques Derrida's Politics of Mourning," to Derrida's *The Work of Mourning* (Chicago: University of Chicago Press, 2001, hereafter cited in text as WM) (*Chaque fois unique, la fin du monde* [Paris: Galilée, 2003]), they write: "As Derrida has shown in numerous texts, the name is always related to death, to the structural possibility that the one who gives, receives,

or bears the name will be absent from it" (13). Brault and Naas also draw our attention to an important passage in Chapter 8, "A Demi-Mot," in which Derrida contends that "[t]he name races toward death even more quickly than we do, we who naively believe we bear it. It bears us with infinite speed toward the end. It is in advance a name of a dead person" (130).

8. In the revised and expanded French version of "Psyché: Invention de l'autre," Derrida underscores the absolute alterity of the child, who always exceeds the most powerful projection of parental narcissism, when he writes: "L'enfant qui parle, interroge, demande avec zèle (studium), est-ce le fruit d'une invention? Invente-t-on un enfant? Si l'enfant s'invente, est-ce comme la projection spéculaire du narcissme parentale ou comme l'autre qui, à parler, à répondre, devant l'invention absolue, la transcendence irréductible du plus proche, d'autant plus hétérogène et inventive qu'elle paraît répondre au désir parental?" *Psyché, Invention de l'autre, t. 1 (nouvelle édition augmentée)* (Paris: Galilée, 1998), 14; "Psyche: Inventions of the Other," trans. Catherine Porter in *Reading De Man Reading*, ed. Lindsay Waters and Wlad Godzich (Minneapolis: University of Minnesota Press, 1989), 27 (hereafter cited in text as PSY).

9. In Derrida's gloss, or, as he calls it, "an aporetic postscript," on Freud's "A Difficulty in the Path of Psycho-analysis," trans. James Strachey, in *The Standard Edition of the Complete Psychological Works of Sigmund Freud*, vol. 17 (London: Hogarth, 1957); "Eine Schweirigkeit der Psychoanalyse" in *Gesammelte Werke* (Bd. XII), he recounts Freud's "comparative history of the three traumas inflicted on human narcissism when it is thus de-centered" (SM 97/161). Derrida elaborates:

"[T]he *psychological* trauma (the power of the unconscious over the conscious ego, discovered by psychoanalysis), after the *biological* trauma (the animal descent of man discovered by Darwin—to whom, moreover, Engels alludes in the Preface to the 1888 *Manifesto*), after the *cosmological* trauma (the Copernican Earth is no longer the center of the universe, and this is more and more the case one could say as to draw from it many consequences concerning the limits of geopolitics). Our aporia would here stem from the fact that there is no longer any name or teleology for determining the Marxist *coup* and its subject. Freud thought he knew, for his part, what man and his narcissism were [. . .]. For we know that the *blow* struck enigmatically in the name of Marx also accumulates and gathers together the other three" (SM 97–98/161–62). There is a temptation on my part to add another postscript to this postscript. It is true that, with no small amount of narcissism, Freud credits himself with striking the third and most devastating blow to human narcissism. In addition to his scandalous theory of infantile sexuality, Freud claims in "A Difficulty in the Path of Psycho-analysis" that the psychological blow that he inflicted to man's self-love by discovering the unconscious—that is to say, that *"the ego is not master in his own house"*—was by far the most traumatic in human history (SE XVII:143). The injury that Freud inflicts on human narcissism quite naturally causes a profound resistance to his thought, a resistance that is more emotional than theoretical. Thus, Freud sums up the difficulty many have with his thought: "I will say at once that it is not an intellectual difficulty I am thinking of, not anything that makes psycho-analysis hard for the reader to understand, but an affective one—something that alienates the feeling of those who come into contact with it, so they become less inclined to believe in it or take interest in it" (SE XVII:137).

One could make the case that it is the Derridean *coup*, with his thinking of *différance*, trace, *pharmakon*, autoimmunity, etc., which has struck the most devastating blow to human narcissism. If we were to write the name of Derrida over that of Marx—"Our aporia would here stem from the fact that there is no longer any name or teleology for determining the Derridean *coup* and its subject"—then we would be able to explain, as Freud attempted to do in his own case, the powerful and affective resistance to Derrida's thought, which leaves no narcissism, in its innumerable guises, unscathed.

For a fascinating interpretation of the above outlined "blows" to man's self-love, see Simon Glendinning's "The End of the World Designed with Men in Mind" forthcoming in the *Journal of Historical Sociology*.

10. The translation has been modified to reflect the revised French edition of this essay.

11. Jacques Derrida, "Portrait d'un philosophe: Jacques Derrida" in *Philosophie, Philosophie* (Revue des Etudiants de Philosophie Université Paris VIII, Vincennes à Saint-Denis), 1997 (hereafter cited in

text as POR). All translations of this text are my own. "Portrait d'un philosophe" will be treated fully in Chapter 5, "An Allegory of Deconstruction" and "Assisting Narcissus."

12. The text for "'There Is No *One* Narcissism' (Autobiophotographies)" published in *Points . . .* is the transcript of a radio interview, entitled "Le bon plaisir de Jacques Derrida," which was conducted by Didier Cahen for France-Culture on March 22, 1986.

13. For example, see Freud's "On Narcissism: An Introduction" and Levinas's "Philosophy and the Idea of the Infinite," in particular the section entitled "Narcissism, or the Philosophy of the Same," in Adriaan Peperzak's *To the Other: An Introduction to the Philosophy of Emmanuel Levinas* (West Lafayette, Ind.: Purdue University Press, 1993).

14. Jacques Derrida, "Mnemosyne," trans. Cecile Lindsay in *Memoires: For Paul de Man*, 2nd rev. ed., trans.Cecile Lindsay, Jonathan Culler, Eduardo Cadava, and Peggy Kamuf (New York: Columbia University Press, 1989), 32 (hereafter cited in text as MP); *Mémoires—pour Paul de Man* (Paris: Galilée, 1988), 52.

5. THE EYE OF NARCISSUS

1. It is important to note the complexity of rendering the various resonances of the French word *exposer*, with which Rogozinski is playing. The verb *exposer* usually connotes "putting on show" or "putting on view," as in a window display or at an art gallery. Hence, the French noun for the putting objects on show is *l'exposition*. In this way, *l'exposition* functions similarly to the English noun "exhibition." However, it is the French verb *exhiber*, meaning "to show off," "to flaunt," etc., that bears the pejorative connotations that are folded in the English word "exhibit" ("to make an exhibit of oneself") and its close relatives ("exhibitionist"). More abstractly, *exposer* can indicate the act of presenting, in order, ideas or facts—*un exposé*. Lastly, *exposer* can, like the English verb "expose," denote an open, vulnerable position of a person or thing. Thus, *exposer* is able to bring together the notions of putting on show and the presentation of ideas with the danger of such exposure. All of these senses of the term are clearly at issue at the Odéon Theater.

2. Derrida further elaborates on his discomfort when confronted with his likeness: "I cannot bear my image. I cannot bear photographs,

I cannot stand television, but above all the horror that I experience when, just by accident, I happen to see an image of me speaking when I have allowed myself to be filmed while presenting a paper [. . .], it is absolute torture" (POR 11).

3. Although Derrida experiences so much unease when catching a glimpse of himself in photographs and on film, he seems to be less embarrassed by seeing his image in sketches or paintings. Despite his discomfort, Derrida submitted to the gaze of numerous artists (painters, photographers, and filmmakers alike). And I believe that he would have insisted to each one, each time: "You have trans-figured me!" Quite literally the artist gives him another figure, and perhaps, as Derrida has shown in *Memoirs of the Blind*, it is the fig-ure of the artist herself. And how does Derrida respond to the other who has transfigured him? In the same manner that he replied to the female artist who rendered a portrait of him that appears in *Derrida* (the movie), by saying "*J'accepte.*" In accepting how the other sees him, Derrida's narcissism necessarily finds itself wounded. Yet, he knows that the only narcissism possible is one that the other gives him as a gift. To the young artist, Derrida says "I can only say I accept [. . .]. It is a very nice gift that she has given me [. . .] that she has given to a little Narcissus." Turning away with a slightly embarrassed smile, he adds "an old Narcissus." See *Derrida*, a film by Kirby Dick and Amy Ziering Kofman (New York: Zeitgeist Films, 2002) (references to the dialogue of the film hereafter cited in text as DM).

4. Derrida defines "allegory" as "that which speaks otherwise with the voice of another" (POR 10). This definition of allegory will also be relevant to our reading of the figure of Echo in Chapter 6, "The Ear of Echo."

5. See David Farrell Krell's *The Purest of Bastards: Works of Mourn-ing, Art, and Affirmation in the Thought of Jacques Derrida* (University Park: Pennsylvania State University Press, 2000), in particular, Chapter 2, "Echo, Narcissus, Echo."

6. *Memoirs of the Blind: The Self-portrait and Other Ruins,* trans. Pascale-Anne Brault and Michael Naas (Chicago: Chicago University Press, 1993), 53; *Mémoires d'aveugle: l'autoportrait et autres ruines* (Paris: Réunion des Musées nationaux, 1990), 157 (hereafter cited in text as MB).

7. See plate no. 7 in *Memoirs of the Blind.*

8. Sigmund Freud, "Mourning and Melancholy," trans. James Strachey in *The Standard Edition of the Complete Psychological Works of Sigmund Freud*, vol. 14 (London: Hogarth, 1957); "Trauer und Melancholie," *Studienausgabe* vol. 3, ed. Alexander Mitscherlich, Angela Richards, and James Strachey (Frankfurt: S. Fischer Verlag, 1969–75). Although this article was written in 1915, not long after "On Narcissism: An Introduction," it only appeared in print in 1917.

9. Jacques Derrida, *The Ear of Other: Otobiography, Transference, Translation*, ed. Christie MacDonald, trans. Peggy Kamuf (Lincoln: University of Nebraska Press, 1985), 57; *L'oreille de l'autre* (Montreal: Vɪb Editeur, 1982) (hereafter cited in text as EO).

10. Jacques Derrida, "Fors: The Anglish Words of Nicholas Abraham and Maria Torok," trans. Barbara Johnson in Nicolas Abraham and Maria Torok, *The Wolf Man's Magic Word: A Cryptonomy*, trans. Nicholas Rand (Minneapolis: University of Minnesota Press, 1986); "Fors: Les mots angles de Nicholas Abraham and Maria Torok " in *Le verbier de l'homme aux loups* (Paris: Flammarion, 1976) (hereafter cited in text as F). Nicholas Abraham and Maria Torok, *The Shell and the Kernal*, ed. and trans. Nicolas T. Rand (Chicago: University of Chicago Press, 1994); *L'écorce et le noyau* (Paris: Flammarion, 1987 [1978]) (hereafter cited in text as SK).

11. See Penelope Deutscher's article "Mourning the Other, Cultural Cannibalism, and the Politics of Friendship (Jacques Derrida and Luce Irigaray)" *Differences* 10, no. 3 (1998):165 (hereafter cited in text as Deutscher).

12. See Elissa Marder's *The Mother in the Age of Mechanical Reproduction: Psychoanalysis, Photography, Deconstruction* (New York: Fordham University Press, 2012), Chapter 1, "The Sex of Death and the Maternal Crypt" and, esp. Chapter 2, "Mourning, Magic, and Telepathy," which insightfully rereads Derrida's appropriation of Abraham and Torok's account of normal and pathological mourning and skillfully shows how, for Derrida, "[t]he subject 'after deconstruction' is produced by the crypt and remains inhabited and haunted by its innumerable unnamed and unnamable encrypted others" (45).

13. In addition to Marder's recent book, essential reading on mourning and Derrida includes the following: Geoffrey Bennington, *Not Half No End: Militantly Melancholic Essay in Memory of*

Jacques Derrida (Edinburgh: Edinburgh University Press, 2010); Sean Gaston, *The Impossible Mourning of Jacques Derrida* (New York: Continuum, 2006); Peggy Kamuf, *To Follow: The Wake of Jacques Derrida* (Edinburgh: Edinburgh University Press, 2010); J. Hillis Miller, *For Derrida* (New York: Fordham University Press, 2009); Michael Naas, *Derrida from Now On* (New York: Fordham University Press, 2008); Kas Saghafi, *Apparitions—Of Derrida's Other* (New York: Fordham University Press, 2010); Nicholas Royle, *In Memory of Jacques Derrida* (Edinburgh: Edinburgh University Press, 2009).

14. A thorough engagement with Derrida's reading of Abraham (originally trained as a Husserlian) and Torok in "Fors" and his deployment of this topology of "the *other* 'in me'" would necessitate not simply a psychoanalytic reading but also a phenomenological account of the relation of the "self" to the "other," which is beyond the scope of the present work.

15. Even the Humanities' website in memory of Derrida at the University of California, Irvine (www.humanities.uci.edu/remembering_jd/) bore this quote as its epigraph, followed by Derrida's photographic image and the (virtual) signatures of thousands who have inscribed a mark of their own loss.

16. Jacques Derrida and Elisabeth Roudinesco, *For What Tomorrow . . . A Dialogue,* trans. Jeff Fort (Palo Alto, Calif.: Stanford University Press, 2004), 160; *De quoi demain . . . Dialogue* (Paris: Fayard/Galilée, 2001), 258 (hereafter cited in text as WT).

17. I read these words by Derrida—"*Il faut bien, il faut* bien *oublier le mort*"—through his comments on Sarah Kofman's last work, "Conjuring Death," in his untitled homage to her. In his interpretation of Kofman's brief, unfinished essay, Derrida insists that "Sarah Kofman seems to sense in this repression [that of the doctors in Rembrandt's *The Anatomy Lesson of Nicholas Tulp*], "in a no doubt very Nietzschean fashion a cunning affirmation of life, its irrepressible movement to survive, to live on [*survivre*]" (WM 176/217). The necessity of the forgetting of the dead, of which Derrida speaks, must be understood as he understood "repression" in Kofman, as a "lie" told in the name of life, in the affirmation of life, "to get, in a word, the better of life" (WM 176/217).

18. See WM 170/210.

19. For an original analysis of the gaze of the other and its relationship to mourning and the image, see Chapter 3, "'*Ça*' *me regarde*: Regarding Responsibility in Derrida," and Chapter 4, "The Ghost of Jacques Derrida," in Saghafi's *Apparitions—Of Derrida's Other*.

20. One must be careful not to conflate "th[is] being 'in us' of the other, in bereaved memory" with some belief in the resurrection of the other *himself*—for, "the other is dead and nothing can save him from this death, nor can anyone save us from it" (MP 21–22/43).

21. For another treatment of Derrida's crucial sentence—"I mourn therefore I am, I am—dead with the death of the other"—see Elissa Marder's "Mourning, Magic, Telepathy" in *The Mother in the Age of Mechanical Reproduction: Psychoanalysis, Photography, Deconstruction*.

22. If mourning—the interminable work of mourning—can be gotten over, it is "by getting over, by ourselves, the mourning of ourselves, I mean the mourning of our autonomy, of everything that would make us the measure of ourselves" (WM 161/200).

23. In Safaa Fathy's film *D'ailleurs Derrida* (La Sept ARTE/Gloria Films, 1999); *Derrida's Elsewhere* (New York: First Run/Icarus, 1999), Derrida confesses to the camera: "I must say, though I've written and published a good deal, I still can't defend myself against a burst of laughter or an expression of modesty. 'Why do you write? You seem to think it's interesting. You take it to your publisher, you write therefore you think it is interesting.' In a way, such an act is absolutely obscene. The act of writing is unjustifiable from that point of view. So you beg pardon, like someone stripping off. 'There, look, I'm exposing myself.' And naturally you ask for forgiveness right away. 'Sorry for showing off.' So, whenever I write, I say sorry to the other [. . .] for the impropriety of writing." The English text for the film transcript was found on Dr. Paul Beidler's web page: www.lrc.edu/eng/Derrida/Elsewhere.htm.

24. In *Dissemination*, the language of *assister* is clearly inflected quite differently than at the Odéon Theater, several decades later: "The attending discourse [*le discours d'assistance*]—which is proliferating here—is addressed to the spectator (who attends the spectacle and is carefully attended in his attendance) and assists him in his reading" (D 325/361).

6. THE EAR OF ECHO

1. Derrida insists that "[i]f one wants to reconstruct a concept of the subject 'after deconstruction,' [. . .] one has to shape a logic and a topic that are rather powerful, supple, articulated, and that therefore can be disarticulated" (PS 321/331–32). It is our contention that in the Derridean reading of Echo, one finds such a supple logic and topic of the "subject," which can be both articulated and disarticulated.

2. Jacques Derrida, *On Touching—Jean-Luc Nancy*, trans. Christine Irizarry (Palo Alto, Calif.: Stanford University Press, 2005), 291; *Le toucher, Jean-Luc Nancy* (Paris: Galilée, 2000), 327 (hereafter cited in text as OT).

3. Jacques Derrida, *Prégnances: Lavis de Colette Deblé, Peintures* (Mont-de-Marsan: L'Atelier des Brisants, 2004).

4. In Derrida's Echo, we hear resonances of Sarah Kofman's interpretation of Plato's "Penia." We refer the reader to Kofman's "Beyond Aporia?" in *Post-structuralist Classics*, trans. David Macey, ed. Andrew E. Benjamin (New York: Routledge, 1988).

5. Jacques Derrida and Bernard Stiegler, *Echographies of Television: Filmed Interviews*, trans. Jennifer Bajorek (Cambridge, UK: Polity Press, 2002), 111; *Échographies de la television. Entretiens filmés* (Paris: Galilée, 1996), 124 (hereafter cited in text as E).

6. Unlike others, in particular Lacan, Derrida does not draw any formal distinction between need and desire. "One must eat well— here is a maxim whose modalities and contents need only be varied, ad infinitum. This evokes a law of need or desire (I have never believed in the radicality of this occasionally useful distinction), *orexis*, hunger and thirst" (PS 282/297).

7. This mimetic interiorization precedes all fiction as such; because "it is," in Derrida's estimation, "the origin of fiction, of apocryphal figuration" (MP 34/54).

8. Jacques Derrida, *Monolingualism of the Other; or, The Prosthesis of Origin*, trans. Patrick Mensah (Palo Alto, Calif.: Stanford University Press, 1998), 66; *Le monolingualism de l'autre ou le prothèse d'origine* (Paris: Galilée, 1996), 125 (hereafter cited in text as MO).

9. It is important to note that Derrida's notion of ex-appropriation is not anthropocentric, as it is not exclusive to human animal. None-

theless, he writes, "the relation to the self in ex-appropriation is radically different (that is why it requires a thinking of difference and not of opposition) in the case of what one calls the 'nonliving,' the 'vegetal,' the 'animal,' 'man,' or 'God'" (PS 269/284).

10. It is the "'logic' of the trace or of difference," Derrida argues, that "determines this re-appropriation as an ex-appropriation," which inevitably "produces the opposite of what it apparently aims for" (PS 269/283).

11. In a footnote in *Rogues*, Derrida cites several translations of Ovid's Latin text ("'[E]cquis adest?' et 'adest' responderat Echo. / hic stupet, utque aciem partes dimittit in omnis, / voce 'veni!' magna clamat: vocat illa vocantem"), in order to demonstrate the impossibility of translation and to show how it "require[es] each time an idiomatic reinvention of the simulacrum in each language" (162n4). As examples, he offers several renderings—two French and one English:

"'*N'y a-t-il pas quelqu'un ici?'*—'*Si, quelqu'un,*' *avait répondu Echo. Narcisse stupéfait porte ses regards de tous côtés:* '*Viens*' *crie-t-il à pleine voix. A son appel répond un appeal d'Echo,* '*Viens*'" (Ovide, *Les Métamorphoses*, trans. Joseph Chamonard [Paris: Garnier-Flammarion, 1966], 99).

"'*Y a-t-il quelqu'un près de moi?*' '*Moi*' *répondit Echo. Plein de stupeur, il promène de tous côtés ses regards.* '*Viens*' *crie-t-il à pleine voix. A son appel répond par un appel*" (Ovide, *Les Métamorphoses*, trans. George Lafaye [Paris: Budé, 1961], I:81–82).

"'Is anyone here?' and 'Here!' cried Echo back. Amazed, he looks around in all directions and with loud voice cries 'Come!'; and 'Come!' she calls him calling" (Ovid, *Metamorphoses*, trans. Frank Justus Miller [Cambridge, Mass.: Harvard University Press, 1984], I:151).

12. I have reproduced here an important passage from *Monolingualism* that links together the uniqueness or singularity of an idiom with the "to come." Derrida writes: "This appeal to come gathers language together in advance. It welcomes it, collects it, not in its identity or unity, not even in its ipseity, but in the uniqueness or singularity of a gathering together of its difference to itself: in difference *with itself* [*avec soi*] rather than *from itself* [*d'avec soi*]. It is not possible to speak outside this promise that gives *a* language, the

uniqueness of an idiom, but only by promising to give it. There can be no question of getting out of this *uniqueness without unity*. It is not to be opposed to the other, nor even distinguished from the other. It is a monolanguage *of* the other" (MO 67–8/127).

13. If each and every appropriation is an ex-appropriation, then the "singularity of the 'who' is not the individuality of a thing that would be identical to itself, it is not an atom. It is a singularity that dislocates or divides itself in gathering itself together to answer to the other, whose call somehow precedes its own identification with itself" (PS 261/276).

14. Little scholarly attention has been paid to the intimate and critical relationship between love and deconstruction; more precisely, to deconstruction as love. See Peggy Kamuf, *Book of Addresses* (Palo Alto, Calif.: Stanford University Press: 2005), 26 (hereafter cited in text as K). Also, on deconstruction and love, see Nicholas Royle's *After Derrida* (Manchester: Manchester University Press, 1995).

Bibliography

Abraham, Nicolas, and Maria Torok. *The Shell and the Kernel: Renewals of Psychoanalysis.* Edited and translated by Nicolas T. Rand. Chicago: University of Chicago Press, 1994. Originally published as *L'écorce et le noyau* (Reprint, Paris: Flammarion, 1987).

Anzieu, Didier. *The Skin Ego.* Translated by Chris Turner. New Haven, Conn.: Yale University Press, 1989. Originally published as *Le moi-peau* (Paris: Dunod, 1985).

Aquinas, Thomas. *On Love and Charity: Readings from the Commentary on Sentences of Peter Lombard.* Translated by Pater A. Kwasniewski, Thomas Bolin, and Joseph Bolin. Washington, D.C.: Catholic University of America, 2008.

Aristotle. *Nicomachean Ethics.* Translated by H. Rackham. Cambridge, Mass.: Harvard University Press, 1934.

Augustine. *City of God against the Pagans.* 7 vols. Translated by W. M. Green, G. E. McCracken, P. Levine, and E. M. Sandford. Cambridge, Mass.: Harvard University Press, 1957–72.

Beardsworth, Sara, *Julia Kristeva: Psychoanalysis and Modernity.* Albany: State University of New York Press, 2004.

Beauvoir, Simone de. *The Second Sex.* Translated by Deirdre Bair. New York: Vintage, 1989. Originally published as *Le deuxième sexe,* tome I and II (Paris: Gallimard, 1949).

Bennington, Geoffrey. *Not Half No End: Militantly Melancholic Essays in Memory of Jacques Derrida*. Edinburgh: Edinburgh University Press, 2010.

Brault, Pascale-Anne, and Michael Naas, "To Reckon with the Dead: Jacques Derrida's Politics of Mourning." Editors' introduction to *The Work of Mourning*, by Jacques Derrida. Translated by Anne-Pascale Brault and Michael Naas. Edited by Anne-Pascale Brault and Michael Naas. Chicago: University of Chicago Press, 2001.

Brint, E. "Echoes of Narcissus." *Political Theory* 16, no. 4 (Nov. 1988): 617–35.

Chase, Cynthia. "Primary Narcissism and the Giving of Figure: Kristeva with Hertz and de Man." In *Abjection, Melancholia, and Love: The Work of Julia Kristeva*. Edited by Andrew Benjamin and John Fletcher. London: Routledge, 1990.

Chazan, Pauline. "Rousseau as Psycho-Social Moralist: The Distinction Between *Amour de soi* and *Amour-propre*." *History of Philosophy Quarterly* 10, no. 4 (October 1993): 341–54.

Cooper, Lawrence. "Between Eros and Will to Power: Rousseau and 'The Desire to Extend Our Being.'" *The American Political Science Review* 98, no. 1 (Feb. 2004): 105–19.

deMan, Paul. *Allegories of Reading: Figural Language in Rousseau, Nietzsche, Rilke, and Proust*. New Haven, Conn.: Yale University Press, 1979.

Dent, NJH. *A Rousseau Dictionary*. Cambridge, Mass.: Blackwell, 1992.

————. "Rousseau on *Amour-propre*." *Proceedings of the Aristotelian Society* 71, no. 2 (1998): 56–73.

Derrida, Jacques. "A Certain Impossible Possibility of Saying the Event." Translated by Gila Walker. *Critical Inquiry* 33 (2007): 441–61. Originally published as "Une certaine possibilité impossible de dire l'événement." In *Dire l'événement, est-ce possible? Seminaire de Montreal, pour Jacques Derrida*, avec Gad Soussana et Alexis Nouss. Paris: L'Harmattan, 2001.

————. *Aporias*. Translated by Thomas Dutoit. Palo Alto, Calif.: Stanford University Press, 1993. *Apories*. Paris: Galilée, 1996.

————. "Deconstructions: The Im-possible." Translated by Michael Taormina. In *French Theory in America*. Edited by Sylvère Lotringer and Sande Cohen. (New York: Routledge, 2001).

———. *Dissemination.* Translated by Barbara Johnson. Chicago: University of Chicago Press, 1981. Originally published as *La Dissémination* (Paris: Seuil, 1972).

———. *The Ear of the Other: Otobiography, Transference, Translation.* Edited by Christie McDonald. Translated by Peggy Kamuf. Lincoln: University of Nebraska Press, 1985. Originally published as *L'oreille de l'autre* (Montreal: Vlb Editeur, 1982).

———. "Fors: The Anglish Words of Nicholas Abraham and Maria Torok." Translated by Barbara Johnson. In *The Wolf Man's Magic Word: A Cryptonomy,* by Nicholas Abraham and Maria Torok. Translated by Nicholas Rand. Minneapolis: University of Minnesota Press, 1986. Originally published as "Fors: Les mots anglés de Nicholas Abraham and Maria Torok." In *Le verbier de l'homme aux loups* (Paris: Flammarion, 1976).

———. *H. C. for Life, That Is to Say.* . . . Translated by Laurent Milesi and Stefan Herbrechter. Palo Alto, Calif.: Stanford University Press, 2006 *H. C. pour la vie, c'est a dire.* . . . (Paris; Galilée, 2002.)

———. "Introduction." In *Sarah Kofman, Selected Writings.* Translated by Pascale-Anne Brault and Michael Naas. Edited by Thomas Albrecht, Georgia Albert, and Elizabeth Rottenberg. Palo Alto, Calif.: Stanford University Press, 2007.

———. *Of Grammatology.* Translated by Gayatry Chakravorty Spivak. Baltimore: Johns Hopkins University Press, 1976. Originally published as *De la grammatologie* (Paris: Minuit, 1967).

———. *Memoirs of the Blind: The Self-Portrait and Other Ruins.* Translated by Pascale-Anne Brault and Michael Naas. Chicago: Chicago University Press, 1993. Originally published as *Mémoires d'aveugle: l'autoportrait et autres ruines* (Paris: Réunion des Musées nationaux, 1990).

———. "Mnemosyne." Translated by Cecile Lindsay. In *Memoires: For Paul de Man,* 2nd rev. ed. Translated by Cecile Lindsay, Jonathan Culler, Eduardo Cadava, and Peggy Kamuf. New York: Columbia University Press, 1989. Originally published as *Mémoires—pour Paul de Man* (Paris: Galilée, 1988).

———. *Monolingualism of the Other; or, The Prosthesis of Origin.* Translated by Patrick Mensah. Palo Alto, Calif.: Stanford University Press, 1998. Originally published as *Le monolinguisme de l'autre ou le prothèse d'origine* (Paris; Galilée, 1996).

————. "Passions: 'An Oblique Offering.'" Translated by David Wood. In *Derrida: A Critical Reader*. Edited by David Wood. Cambridge, Mass.: Blackwell, 1992. Originally published as *Passions* (Paris: Galilée, 1993).

————. "Portrait d'un philosophe: Jacques Derrida." In *Philosophie, Philosophie* (Revue des Etudiants de Philosophie Université Paris VIII, Vincennes à Saint-Denis, 1997).

————. *Prégnances: Lavis de Colette Deblé, Peintures*. Mont-de-Marsan: L'Atelier des Brissants, 2004.

————. *Psyché, Invention de l'autre, t. 1 (nouvelle édition augmentée)*. Paris: Galilée, 1998. Translated by Catherine Porter as "Psyche: Inventions of the Other." In *Reading De Man Reading*. Edited by Lindsay Waters and Wlad Godzich. (Minneapolis: University of Minnesota Press, 1989).

————. *Rogues: Two Essays on Reason*. Translated by Pascale-Anne Brault and Michael Naas. Palo Alto, Calif.: Stanford University Press, 2005. Originally published as *Voyous: Deux essays sur la raison* (Paris: Galilée, 2003).

————. *Specters of Marx: The State of the Debt, the Work of Mourning, and the New International*. Translated by Peggy Kamuf. New York: Routledge, 1994. Originally published as *Spectres de Marx: l'état de la dette, le travail du deuil et la nouvelle international* (Paris: Galilée, 1993).

————. "'There Is No *One* Narcissism' (Autobiophotographies)." Translated by Peggy Kamuf in *Points . . . : Interviews, 1974–1994*. Selected and presented by Elisabeth Weber. Palo Alto, Calif. Stanford University Press, 1995. Originally published as *Points de suspension: Entretiens* (Paris: Galilée, 1992).

————. *On Touching—Jean-Luc Nancy*. Translated by Christine Irizarry. Palo Alto, Calif.: Stanford University Press, 2005. Originally published as *Le toucher, Jean-Luc Nancy* (Paris: Galilée, 2000).

————. *The Work of Mourning*. Edited by Pascale-Anne Brault and Michael Naas. Chicago: University of Chicago Press, 2001. Originally published as *Chaque fois unique, la fin du monde* (Paris: Galilée, 2003).

Derrida, Jacques, with Marie-Françoise Plissart. *Right of Inspection*. Translated by David Wills. New York: Monacelli Press, 1998. Originally published as *Droit de regard* (Paris: Minuit, 1985).

Derrida, Jacques, and Elisabeth Roudinesco. *For What Tomorrow . . . A Dialogue.* Translated by Jeff Fort. Palo Alto, Calif.: Stanford University Press, 2004. Originally published as *De quoi demain . . . Dialogue* (Paris: Fayard/Galilée, 2001).

Derrida, Jacques, and Bernard Stiegler. *Echographies of Television: Filmed Interviews.* Translated by Jennifer Bajorek. Cambridge, UK: Polity Press, 2002. Orginally published as *Échographies de la television. Entretiens filmés* (Paris: Galilée, 1996).

Deutscher, Penelope. "Mourning the Other, Cultural Cannibalism, and the Politics of Friendship (Jacques Derrida and Luce Irigaray)." *Differences* 10, no. 3 (1998): 159–84.

Dick, Kirby, and Amy Ziering Kofman. *Derrida* (movie). Zeitgeist Films, New York, 2002.

Fathy, Safaa. *D'ailleurs Derrida.* La Sept ARTE/Gloria Films, 2000. *Derrida's Elsewhere.* First Run/Icarus, New York, 1999.

Force, Pierre. "Self-love, Identification, and the Origin of Political Economy." Edited by Elena Russo. *Yale French Studies*, no. 92, *Exploring the Conversable World* (1997): 46–64.

Freud, Sigmund. "A Difficulty in the Path of Psycho-analysis." In vol. 17 of *The Standard Edition of the Complete Psychological Works of Sigmund Freud.* Translated by James Strachey. London: Hogarth, 1957.

———. *The Ego and the Id.* In vol. 19 of *The Standard Edition of the Complete Psychological Works of Sigmund Freud.* Translated by James Strachey. London: Hogarth, 1957.

———. *Group Psychology and the Analysis of the Ego.* In vol. 18 of *The Standard Edition of the Complete Psychological Works of Sigmund Freud.* Translated by James Strachey. London: Hogarth Press, 1966.

———. *Leonard da Vinci and a Memory of his Childhood.* In vol. 11 of *The Standard Edition of the Complete Psychological Works of Sigmund Freud.* Translated by James Strachey. London: Hogarth, 1953.

———. "Mourning and Melancholy." In vol. 14 of *The Standard Edition of the Complete Psychological Works of Sigmund Freud.* Translated by James Strachey. London: Hogarth, 1957.

———. "On Narcissism: An Introduction." In vol. 14 of *The Standard Edition of the Complete Psychological Works of Sigmund Freud.* Translated by James Strachey. London: Hogarth, 1957.

————. "Some Psychological Consequences of the Anatomical Distinctions between the Sexes." In vol. 19 of *The Standard Edition of the Complete Psychological Works of Sigmund Freud*. Translated by James Strachey. London: Hogarth, 1957.

————. "The Taboo on Virginity." In vol. 11 of *The Standard Edition of the Complete Psychological Works of Sigmund Freud*. Translated by James Strachey. London: Hogarth, 1953.

————. *Three Essays on Theory of Sexuality*. In vol. 7 of *The Standard Edition of the Complete Psychological Works of Sigmund Freud*. Translated by James Strachey. London: Hogarth, 1957.

Frontisi-Ducroux, Françoise, and Jean-Pierre Vernant. *Dans l'œil du miroir*. Paris: Odile Jacob, 1997.

Gambaudo, Sylvie. *Kristeva, Psychoanalysis and Culture*. Hampshire: Ashgate Publishing, 2007.

Gaston, Sean. *The Impossible Mourning of Jacques Derrida*. New York: Continuum, 2006.

Green, André. *Life Narcissism, Death Narcissism*. Translated by Andrew Weller. London: Free Association Press, 2001. Originally published as *Narcissisme de vie, narcissisme de mort* (Paris: Minuit, 1983).

Kamuf, Peggy. *Book of Addresses*. Palo Alto, Calif.: Stanford University Press: 2005.

————. *To Follow: The Wake of Jacques Derrida*. Edinburgh: Edinburgh University Press, 2010.

Kant, Immanuel. *Lectures on Ethics*. Translated by Louis Infield. Indianapolis: Hackett, 1980.

Kofman, Sarah. "Beyond Aporia?" In *Post-structuralist Classics*. Translated by David Macey. Edited by Andrew E. Benjamin. New York: Routledge, 1988.

————. "Conjuring Death: Remarks on *The Anatomy Lesson of Doctor Nicolas Tulp* (1632)." In *Selected Writings*. Translated by Pascale-Anne Brault. Edited by Thomas Albrecht, Georgia Albert, and Elizabeth Rottenberg. Palo Alto, Calif.: Stanford University Press, 2007.

————. *The Enigma of Woman: Woman in Freud's Writings*. Translated by Catherine Porter. Ithaca, N.Y.: Cornell University Press, 1985. Originally published as *L'énigme de la femme: La femme dans les texts de Freud* (Paris: Galilee, 1980).

Krell, David Farrell. *The Purest of Bastards: Works of Mourning, Art, and Affirmation in the Thought of Jacques Derrida*. University Park: Pennsylvania State University Press, 2000.

Kristeva, Julia. *L'amour de soi et ses avatars. Démesure et limites de la sublimation*. Nantes: Editions Pleins Feux, 2005.

———. *Colette*. Translated by Jane Marie Todd. New York: Columbia University Press, 2004. Originally published as *Le génie féminin: Tome III. Colette* (Paris: Fayard, 2002).

———. *Hannah Arendt*. Translated by Ross Guberman. New York: Columbia University Press, 2001. Originally published as *Le génie féminin: Tome I. Hannah Arendt* (Paris: Fayard, 1999).

———. *In the Beginning Was Love: Psychoanalysis and Faith*. Translated by Arthur Goldhammer. New York: Columbia University Press, 1987. Originally published as *Au commencement était l'amour—psychanalyse et foi* (Paris: Hachette, 1985).

———. "Is There a Feminine Genuis?" *Critical Inquiry* 30 (Spring 2004): 493–504.

———. *Melanie Klein*. Translated by Ross Guberman. New York: Columbia University Press, 2004. Originally published as *Le génie féminin: Tome II. Melanie Klein* (Paris: Fayard, 2000).

———. *Nations without Nationalism*. Translated by Leon S. Roudiez. New York: Columbia University Press, 1993. Originally published as *Lettre ouverte à Harlem Désir* (Paris: Rivages, 1990).

———. *New Maladies of the Soul*. Translated by Ross Guberman. New York: Columbia University Press, 1995. Originally published as *Les nouvelles maladies de l'âme* (Paris: Fayard, 1993).

———. *The Portable Kristeva*. Edited by Kelly Oliver. New York: Columbia University Press, 1997.

———. *Powers of Horror: An Essay on Abjection*. Translated by Leon S. Roudiez. New York: Columbia University Press, 1982. Originally published as *Pouvoirs de l'horreur: Essai sur l'abjection* (Paris: Seuil, 1980).

———. *Revolution in Poetic Language*. Translated by Margaret Waller. New York: Columbia University Press, 1984. Originally published as *La révolution du language poétique* (Paris: Editions du Seuil, 1974).

———. *The Sense and Non-Sense of Revolt: The Powers and Limits of Psychoanalysis, Volume I*. Translated by Jeanine Herman. New York:

Columbia University Press, 2000. Originally published as *Sens et non-sens de la révolte: Pouvoirs et limites de la psychanalyse I* (Paris: Fayard, 1996).

————. *This Incredible Need to Believe.* Translated by Beverley Bie Brahic. New York: Columbia University Press, 2009. Originally published as *Cet incroyable besoin de croire* (Paris: Fayard, 2007).

————. *Tales of Love*, trans. Leon Roudiez. New York: Columbia University Press, 1987. Originally published as *Histoires d'amour* (Paris: Editions Denoël, 1983).

Lacan, Jacques. *Ecrits: A Selection*, Translated by Alan Sheridan. New York: Norton, 1977. Originally published as *Ecrits* (Paris: Seuil, 1966).

Lafond, Jean, ed. *Moralistes du XVIIe Siècle.* Paris: Robert Laffont, 1992.

La Fontaine, Jean de. *Fables.* Paris: Garnier frères, 1960.

Laplanche, Jean, and Jean-Bertrand Pontalis. *The Language of Psychoanalysis.* Translated by Donald Nicholson-Smith. New York: Norton, 1973. Originally published as *Le vocabulaire de psychanalyse* (Paris: Presses Universitaires de France, 1967).

La Rochefoucauld, François de. *Maximes.* Edited by Jacques Truchet. Paris: Garnier-Flammarion, 1977.

Levinas, Emmanuel. "Philosophy and the Idea of the Infinite." In *To the Other: An Introduction to the Philosophy of Emmanuel Levinas*, by Adriaan Peperzak. West Lafayette, Ind.: Purdue University Press, 1993.

MacCannell, Juliet Flower. "Nature and Self-Love: A Reinterpretation of Rousseau's 'Primitive Passion.'" *PMLA* 92, no. 5 (Oct. 1977): 890–902.

Marder, Elissa. *The Mother in the Age of Mechanical Reproduction: Psychoanalysis, Photography, Deconstruction.* New York: Fordham University Press, 2012.

Marin, Louis. *Des pouvoirs de l'image: gloses.* Paris: Seuil, 1993.

Miller, J. Hillis. *For Derrida.* New York: Fordham University Press, 2009.

Naas, Michael. *Derrida from Now On.* New York: Fordham University Press, 2008.

Nygren, Anders. *Agape and Eros.* Translated by Philip S. Watson. Philadelphia: Westminster, 1953. Originally published as *Eros et Agapè.*

La Notion chrétienne de l'amour et ses transformations (Paris: Aubier, 1930, 1962).

O'Hagan, Timothy. "Rousseau on *Amour-Propre*: On Six Facets of *Amour-Propre*." *Proceedings of the Aristotelian Society* 99, no. 1 (1999): 91–108.

Oliver, Kelly. *Family Values: Subjects between Nature and Culture.* New York: Routledge, 1997.

———. *Reading Kristeva: Unraveling the Double-Bind.* Indianapolis: Indiana University Press, 1993.

———. *Subjectivity without Subjects: From Abject Fathers to Desiring Mothers.* Lanham, Md.: Rowman & Littlefield, 1998.

Ovid. *Metamorphoses.* Translated by Allen Mandelbaum. New York: Harvest, 1993.

Pascal, Blaise. *Pensées.* Paris: Garnier-Flammarion, 1976.

Plotinus. *The Enneads.* Translated by Stephen Mackenna. Abridged by John Dillon. New York: Penguin, 1991.

Rousseau, Jean-Jacques. *Emile or On Education.* Introduced, translated, with notes by Allan Bloom. New York: Basic Books, 1979. Originally published as *Oeuvres completes.* Vol. 4. Edited by Bernard Gagnebin, Marcel Raymond, et al. (Paris: NRF-Editions de la Pléiade, 1959–1995).

———. *The First and Second Discourses and Essay on the Origin of Languages.* Edited, translated, and annotated by Victor Gourevitch. New York: Harper & Row, 1986. Originally published as *Oeuvres complètes.* Vol. 3. Edited by Bernard Gagnebin, Marcel Raymond, et al. (Paris: NRF-Editions de la Pléiade, 1959–1995).

———. "Narcissus; or, the Lover of Himself." In *Letter to D'Alembert and Writings for the Theater. The Collected Writings of Rousseau,* vol. 10. Edited and translated by Allan Bloom, Charles Butterworth, and Christopher Kelly. Hanover, N.H.: University Press of New England, 2004. Originally published as *Narcisse ou l'amant de lui-même* in *Oeuvres complètes.* Vol. 2. Edited by Bernard Gagnebin, Marcel Raymond, et al. (Paris: NRF-Editions de la Pléiade, 1959–95).

———. "Preface to Narcissus." In *The First and Second Discourses and Essay on the Origin of Languages.* Edited, translated, and annotated by Victor Gourevitch. New York: Harper & Row, 1986. Originally published as "Préface de *Narcisse*" in *Oeuvres complètes.*

Vol. 2. Edited by Bernard Gagnebin, Marcel Raymond, et al. (Paris: NRF-Editions de la Pléiade, 1959–95).

Royle, Nicholas. *After Derrida.* Manchester: Manchester University Press, 1995.

———. *In Memory of Jacques Derrida.* Edinburgh: Edinburgh University Press, 2009.

Saghafi, Kas. *Apparitions—Of Derrida's Other.* New York: Fordham University Press, 2010.

Vinge, Louise. *The Narcissus Theme in Western European Literature up to the Early 19th Century.* Lund: Gleerups, 1967.

Voltaire. *Le Siècle de Louis XIV.* In *Oeuvres historiques.* Edited by René Pomeau. Paris: Gallimard, 1957, Pléiade edition.

Ziarek, Ewa Plonowska. *An Ethics of Dissensus: Postmodernity, Feminism, and the Politics of Radical Democracy.* Palo Alto, Calif.: Stanford University Press, 2001.

Index